Standards-Based
SOCIAL STUDIES
Graphic Organizers, Rubrics, and Writing Prompts
for Middle Grade Students

By Imogene Forte
and Sandra Schurr

Incentive Publications, Inc.
Nashville, Tennessee

Graphics by Joe Shibley
Cover by Marta Drayton
Edited by Jean K. Signor

ISBN 0-86530-490-4

PRINTED IN THE UNITED STATES OF AMERICA
www.incentivepublications.com

Table of Contents

PREFACE

Recent research studies have confirmed a belief that intuitive teachers have long held germane to classroom success; when students are meaningfully involved in active learning tasks and in the planning and evaluation of their work, they are more enthusiastic about instructional activities, they learn and retain more, and their overall rate of achievement is greater. With the emphasis placed on measurable achievement as an overriding goal driving school system mandates, curriculum, classroom organization and management, and even instructional practices and procedures, teachers are faced with great challenges. While striving to fulfill societal demands, at the same time they must be creating and using new instructional strategies, procedures, and teaching methods to meet the diverse needs of students with widely varying interests and abilities. With the complexity of daily life in the rapidly changing world in which we live, the global economy, and the growing avalanche of information, middle grades social studies teachers are turning to student-centered instruction, active learning strategies, and authentic instruction to capture and hold students' interests and attention, and consequently to result in increased achievement levels.

Graphic Organizers

As the body of material to be covered in a given time frame grows more massive and multifaceted, and content demands on students and teachers multiply, graphic organizers are becoming an important component of middle grades social studies programs.

In the information-saturated classroom of today, sorting and making meaningful use of specific facts, and concepts is becoming an increasingly important skill. Knowing where to go to find information and how to organize it once it is located is the key to processing and making meaningful use of the information gathered. Graphic organizers can be used to: provide visual organization; develop scope and sequence; furnish a plan of action or to aid in assessment; clarify points of interest; and document a process or a series of events.

Their construction and use encourages visual discrimination and organization, use of critical thinking skills, and meta-cognitive reflection. They can be particularly useful in helping middle grade students grasp concepts and skills related to the ten standards established by the National Council of Social Studies.

In other instances, a graphic organizer may be developed as a reporting or review exercise or sometimes as a means of self-assessment when properly used after knowledge has been acquired. Graphic organizers become a valuable and effective instructional and assessment tool. The degree of their effectiveness for both students and teachers is determined by visual clarification of purpose, careful planning, visual organization, and attention to detail.

Rubrics

Authentic assessment, as opposed to more traditional forms of assessment, gives both student and teacher a more realistic picture of gains made, facts, and information processed for retention. Emphasis is placed more on the processing of concepts and information than on the recall of facts. Collecting evidence from authentic assessment exercises, taking place in realistic settings over a period of time, provides students and teachers with the most effective documentation of both skills and content mastery. Traditional measurements of student achievement such as written tests and quizzes, objective end-of-chapter tests, and standardized tests play a major role in the assessment picture as well.

The use of standards-based rubrics in middle grade social studies classes has proven to be an extremely useful means of authentic assessment for helping students maintain interest and evaluate their own progress.

Rubrics are checklists that contain sets of criteria for measuring the elements of a product, performance, or portfolio. They can be designed as a qualitative measure (holistic rubric) to gauge overall performance of a prompt, or they can be designed as a quantitative measure (analytic rubric) to award points for each of several elements in response to a prompt.

Additional benefits from rubrics are that they: require collaboration among students and teachers; are flexible and allow for individual creativity; make room for individual strengths and weaknesses; minimize competition; are meaningful to parents; allow for flexible time frames; provide multifaceted scoring systems with a variety of formats; can be sources for lively peer discussions and interaction; can include meta-cognitive reflection provisions which encourage self-awareness and critical thinking; and can help teachers determine final grades that are understood by and hold meaning for students.

Writing Prompts

Over the past several years, the significance of journals and writing prompts is well-documented by student and teacher observations. When students write about experiences, knowledge, hopes, fears, memories, and dreams, they broaden and clarify skills and concepts while acquiring new insights into themselves and the big world of which they are a part.

While random journal entries hold their own place of importance in the social studies classroom, writing prompts designed to elicit specific responses play a vital role in the instructional program.

Journal entries may be presented in many different formats, and may be shared and assessed in a variety of ways. The flexibility of their use and the possibility they provide for integrating instruction cause them to be viewed as an important component of the personalized social studies program. They may take the form of a file card project, a multimedia presentation, a special notebook, or a diary. They may be private to be discussed with the teacher only, shared with a small group of peers, or the total class. Word prompts can be used in parent-student-teacher conferences, or as take home projects to be shared with parents, saved, or used as a portfolio entry to give an account of a unit of study, field trip, or independent project.

Writing prompts provide the opportunity for students to: create a dialogue with teachers in meaningful sense; write about self-selected topics of high interest; process and internalize material being learned; communicate with peers; express private opinions, thoughts, and insights without judgment or censor; write personal reactions or responses to textbook, research assignments, group discussion, and cooperative learning experiences; make record of what and how they are learning and what it means to them; develop a source book of ideas and thoughts related to a specific topic; question material being studied and record answers as they are uncovered; assess their academic or social progress; and engage in meta-cognitive reflection on new skills and concepts being acquired and record plans for further exploration.

These standards-based graphic organizers, writing prompts, and rubrics have been designed to provide busy teachers with a bank of resources from which to draw as the need arises. The ten standards developed by the National Council of Social Studies have been incorporated throughout all activities. For ease in planning, the matrix on page 132 provides a complete correlation of activities to these standards.

Graphic Organizers

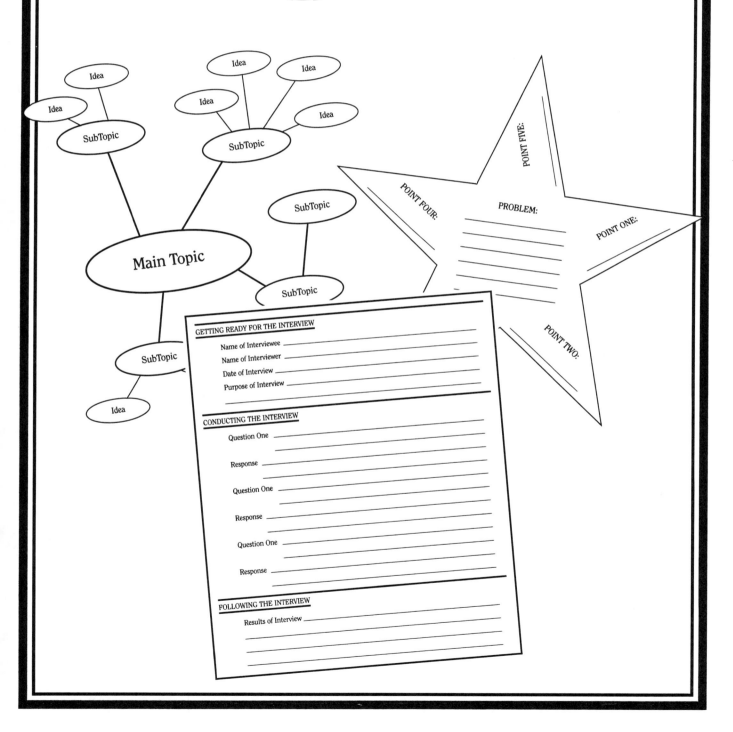

Idea

Idea

SubTopic

Idea

Idea

Idea

SubTopic

Idea

SubTopic

Main Topic

SubTopic

SubTopic

Idea

POINT FIVE:

POINT FOUR:

PROBLEM:

POINT ONE:

POINT TWO:

GETTING READY FOR THE INTERVIEW

Name of Interviewee _____

Name of Interviewer _____

Date of Interview _____

Purpose of Interview _____

CONDUCTING THE INTERVIEW

Question One _____

Response _____

Question One _____

Response _____

Question One _____

Response _____

FOLLOWING THE INTERVIEW

Results of Interview _____

GUIDELINES
FOR USING GRAPHIC ORGANIZERS

1. Graphic organizers have many purposes; they can be used for curriculum planning, helping students process information, and pre- or post-assessment tasks. Determine which types of graphic organizers are best for each purpose.

2. Graphic organizers are a performance-based model of assessment and make excellent artifacts for inclusion in a portfolio. Decide which concepts in your discipline are best represented by the use of these organizers.

3. Use graphic organizers to help students focus on important concepts while omitting extraneous details.

4. Use graphic organizers as visual pictures to help the student remember key ideas.

5. Use graphic organizers to connect visual language with verbal language in active learning settings.

6. Use graphic organizers to enhance recall of important information.

7. Use graphic organizers to provide student motivation and relieve student boredom.

8. Use graphic organizers to show and explain relationships between and among varied content areas.

9. Use graphic organizers to make traditional lesson plans more interactive and more appealing to the visual learner.

10. Use graphic organizers to break down complex ideas through concise and structured visuals.

11. Use graphic organizers to help students note patterns and clarify ideas.

12. Use graphic organizers to help students better understand the concept of part to whole.

13. Emphasize the use of graphic organizers to stimulate creative thinking.

14. Make sure there is a match between the type of organizer and the content being taught.

15. Make sure that using a graphic organizer is the best use of time when teaching a concept.

16. Use a wide variety of graphic organizers and use them collaboratively whenever possible.

Standards-Based SOCIAL STUDIES Graphic Organizers,
Rubrics, and Writing Prompts for Middle Grade Students

Copyright ©2001 by Incentive Publications, Inc.
Nashville, TN.

Bloom's Lesson Plan Outline

Directions: Each of the six levels of Bloom's Taxonomy can be best understood through the use of several types of action verbs or behaviors. Choose from the list below one verb or behavior for each level of the taxonomy and write a task or activity to complete on the Bloom Lesson Plan Outline.

Knowledge level:
    define, list, identify, recall, draw, or recite
Comprehension level:
    explain, summarize, find, measure, or show
Application level:
    discuss, interview, perform, prove, or use
Analysis level:
    Criticize, debate, diagram, examine, search, or sort
Synthesis level:
    create, imagine, produce, propose, or present
Evaluation level:
    assess, defend, judge, recommend, or verify

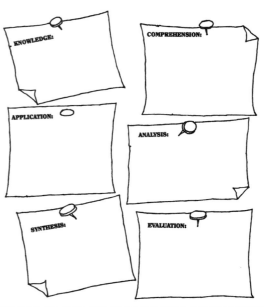

See page 22 for reproducible copy.

Calendar Organizer

Directions: The simple calendar organizer is a valuable organizational tool for use on all content areas. The blank calendar may be used to create a portfolio artifact, to serve as the basis of an outline or a timeline for a project or course of study as a record-keeping device for homework or classroom assignments, as a peer tutoring or cooperative learning aid or as an instructional tool.

See page 23 for reproducible copy.

Standards-Based SOCIAL STUDIES Graphic Organizers, Rubrics, and Writing Prompts for Middle Grade Students

Build A Case

Build A Case is a tool for recording the pros and cons or arguments for and against a given position when studying a controversial problem, issue, or decision.

In each window of the building, the student writes down a series of "pro" or "for" statements and a series of "con" or "against" statements. The doors in and out of the building are used to write down conclusions or solutions to the conflicting statements.

See page 24 for reproducible copy.

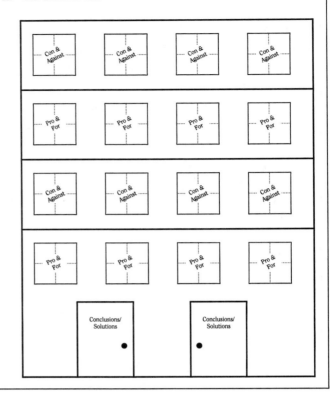

Concept Map

A Concept Map is built around a main idea (or central concept) important to the study of a given topic. Other thoughts related to the main idea in some meaningful way are recorded as extensions or associations of the main concept through a series of adjacent lines and circles.

See page 25 for reproducible copy.

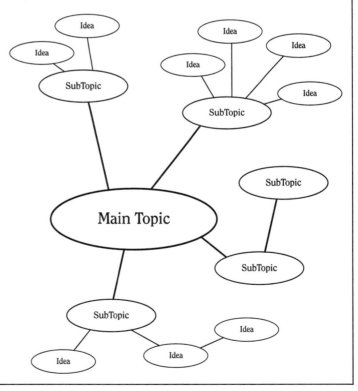

Cultural Heroes

Directions: Choose a specific culture and identify the major players or characters that were important to its activities or outcomes in a significant way.

See page 26 for reproducible copy.

My List Of Heroes	My List Of Decision-Makers	My List Of Victims	My List Of Leaders
My List Of Facilitators	My List Of Conformists	My List Of Troublemakers	My List Of Pacifists

Data Graph

The Data Graph is a tool for collecting and organizing numerical information so that it can be used to draw conclusions and report findings. This organizer can be used to compile data on a variety of topics and to show or display the information using the format of a bar graph, circle graph, line graph, or picture graph.

See page 27 for reproducible copy.

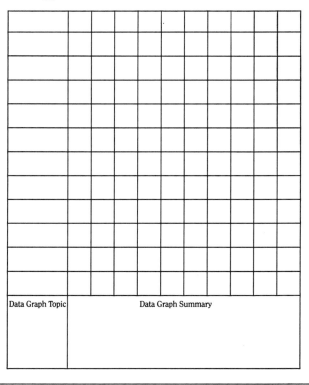

Data Graph Topic   Data Graph Summary

Decision-Making Chart

DIRECTIONS: Use this chart to outline the important decisions that were made during a historical conflict or decision-making situation. Consider optional positions/outcomes and those criteria to be used in evaluating the alternative positions/outcomes.

Record each option as a sentence and each criterion as a question.

Rate each sentence/criteria entry with a plus (+), a minus (-), or a question mark (?).

See page 28 for reproducible copy.

Optional Positions / Outcomes	Criteria To Consider					Rating
1.						
2.						
3.						
4.						
5.						
6.						
Comments						

Event-Tracking Map

DIRECTIONS: Choose an economic-related event and record the key pieces of information in the appropriate places so that you can keep track of the most significant people, places, and actions associated with the event.

See page 29 for reproducible copy.

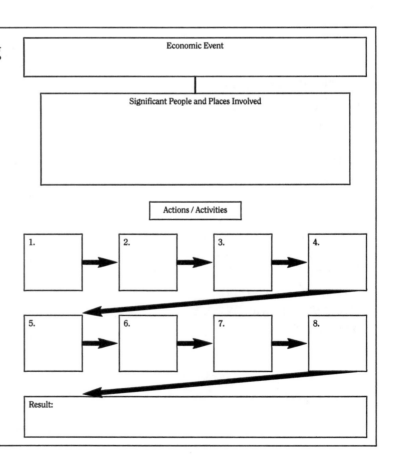

Famous Person Chart

A Famous Person Chart depicts the personality traits, actions, and accomplishments of a well-known historical or famous leader who is described and discussed in the reading of a fiction/nonfiction book, a textbook selection, or a newspaper/magazine article. Important pieces of information are recorded on the outline of the character as a visual record of what this person has accomplished through words, actions, and deeds.

See page 30 for reproducible copy.

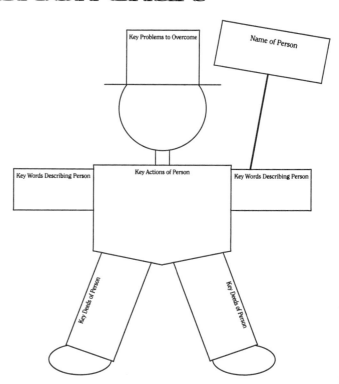

Interdisciplinary Tree

An Interdisciplinary Tree is used to record different kinds of factual information according to specific subject areas that they represent. The main topic of the research is recorded on the tree trunk and then different branches of the tree are designated as facts representing the disciplines of math, science, social studies, art, music, and language.

See page 31 for reproducible copy.

Standards-Based SOCIAL STUDIES Graphic Organizers, Rubrics, and Writing Prompts for Middle Grade Students

Interview Organizer

The Interview Organizer is designed to structure an interview that a student might conduct with another person of interest. It requires an advanced set of questions to be asked by the interviewer, as well as spaces for recording the interviewee's responses.

See page 32 for reproducible copy.

GETTING READY FOR THE INTERVIEW

Name of Interviewee _____

Name of Interviewer _____

Date of Interview _____

Purpose of Interview _____

_____

CONDUCTING THE INTERVIEW

Question One _____

_____

Response _____

_____

Question One _____

_____

Response _____

_____

Question One _____

_____

Response _____

_____

FOLLOWING THE INTERVIEW

Results of Interview _____

_____

_____

_____

KWL Chart

A KWL Chart guides students through a three-step process by recording a series of knowledge-based statements, a set of questions, and items learned as part of a research or reading task. Before investigating a topic, students should write down facts they know in the K column (or What I Know column), questions they hope to find answers to in the W column (or What I Want to Know column), and information learned in the L column (or What I Learned column).

See page 33 for reproducible copy.

Topic of Study _____

Student's Name _____

K What I Know	W What I Want to Know	L What I Learned

Standards-Based SOCIAL STUDIES Graphic Organizers, Rubrics, and Writing Prompts for Middle Grade Students

Maps

Maps provide the student with an outline in a mapping format to draw symbols, icons, shapes, objects, or unique graphics to visually describe a special setting or location. Each map should include a Key complete with designated colors, numbers, or codes for easy interpretation of both scale and knowledge presented.

See page 34 for reproducible copy.

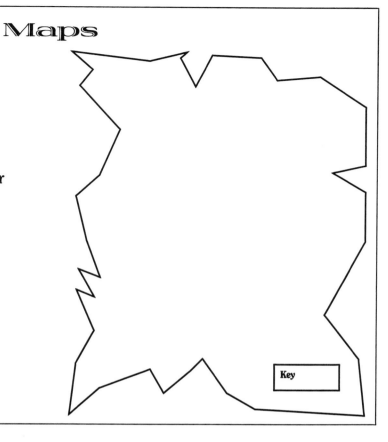

Key

Matrix

A matrix allows the student to both compare and contrast objects according to an established set of variables and then to discover those patterns and relationships that may or may not exist among them. The names of the objects being compared are written down the side of the matrix while the criteria or variables being used are written across the top. A plus (+) for positive correlation can be used in each box or a minus (–) for negative correlation can be used in each box.

See page 35 for reproducible copy.

NAMES OF OBJECTS	Criterion	Criterion	Criterion	Criterion	Criterion	Criterion	Criterion	Criterion	Criterion	Criterion	Criterion	Criterion
1.												
2.												
3.												
4.												
5.												
6.												
7.												
8.												
9.												
10.												
11.												
12.												
13.												
14.												
15.												
16.												
17.												
18.												
19.												
20.												

Standards-Based SOCIAL STUDIES Graphic Organizers, Rubrics, and Writing Prompts for Middle Grade Students

Observation Log

An Observation Log is a collection of simple, but informative entries about a given topic or subject. Observation logs are used to watch something closely over a period of time and to record the changes of what you see during this process. All entries require a date and time for the observation as well as a few lines describing what you see.

See page 36 for reproducible copy.

Picture Puzzle

Picture Puzzle is a graphic organizer that allows students to research a topic and record separate facts or pieces of information gleaned from the readings on individual puzzle pieces. These puzzle pieces can then be reviewed and rewritten into a short report summary.

See page 37 for reproducible copy.

Points To Ponder

Points To Ponder encourages students to consider various points or solutions to a specific problem under study. The problem is written in the center of the star and the key points to consider or potential solutions to the problem are written on the five points of the star.

See page 38 for reproducible copy.

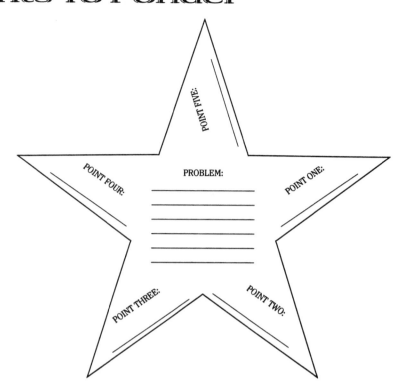

Read-to-Know Chart

Directions: Use the Read-to-Know Chart to record information from the various sections of a social studies or geography textbook. Select a chapter in the text and then write down information you would like to know from each section of the chapter before you read it and then what you learned from the chapter after you read it.

See page 39 for reproducible copy.

Section Title	What I Expect To Learn	What I Learned
1.		
2.		
3.		
4.		
5.		
6.		
7.		
8.		
9.		

Scope and Sequence Map

DIRECTIONS: Record the important steps or events, in chronological order, associated with a problem situation that occurred in history as well as the outcome of those steps or events in finding a solution.

See page 40 for reproducible copy.

Historical Setting

Historical Figures

Historical Problem Situation

First Event/Step: _____

Second Event/Step: _____

Third Event/Step: _____

Fourth Event/Step: _____

Fifth Event/Step: _____

Outcomes: _____

Resolution: _____

Story Board

A storyboard is used to describe a series of events in chronological order. Organize your pieces of information, ideas, thoughts, or situations in a logical sequence based on when and how they occurred. Consider using this organizer to identify events leading up to a conflict, war, election, historical moment, discovery, invention, disaster, or exploration.

See page 41 for reproducible copy.

1.	6.
2.	7.
3.	8.
4.	9.
5.	10.

What, So What, Now What?

A *What, So What, And Now What?* Chart organizes one's thinking after reading a story, textbook section, or an article on a given topic by requiring reflection back over the information presented.

The *What?* column requires the student to write down a response to the question: *What did I learn from this selection?*

The *So What?* column requires the student to write down a series of responses to the question: *What difference does it make now that I know this?*

The *And Now What?* column asks students to write down some thoughts answering the question: *How can I use this information to make a difference in what I know or can do?*

See page 42 for reproducible copy.

Topic of Study _____

Student's Name _____

What?	So What?	And Now What?

Venn Diagram

A Venn Diagram consists of three large intersecting circles that are used to compare and contrast three different, but related, objects, concepts, events, and persons.
The intersecting parts of the circles are used to record common elements of the three items while the outer parts of the circles are used to record elements uniquely appropriate for any one of the circles.

See page 43 for reproducible copy.

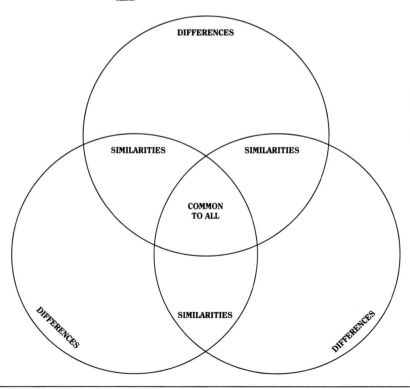

Standards-Based SOCIAL STUDIES Graphic Organizers, Rubrics, and Writing Prompts for Middle Grade Students

Bloom's Lesson Plan Outline

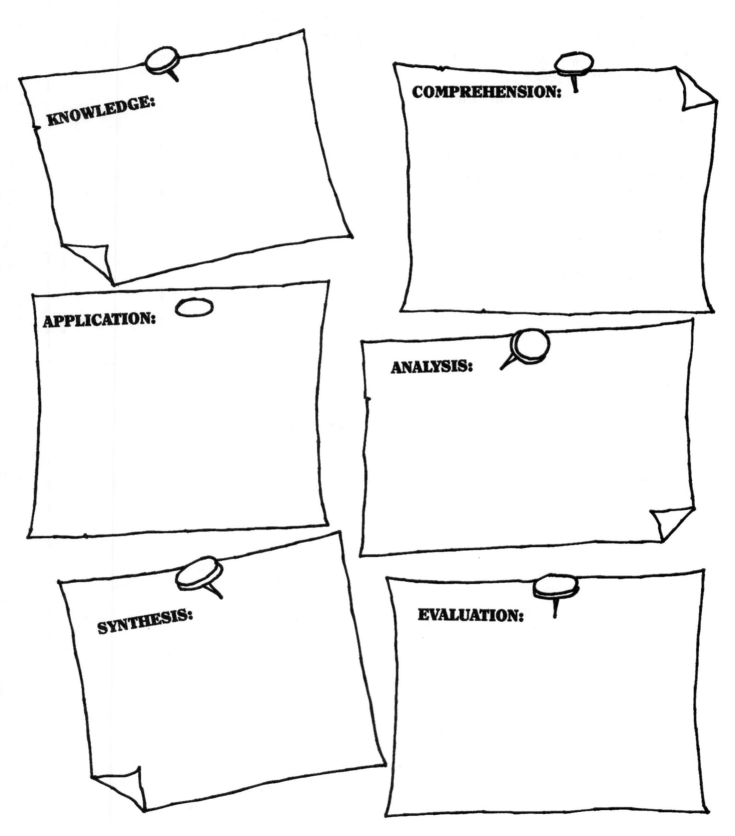

KNOWLEDGE:

COMPREHENSION:

APPLICATION:

ANALYSIS:

SYNTHESIS:

EVALUATION:

Standards-Based SOCIAL STUDIES Graphic Organizers,
Rubrics, and Writing Prompts for Middle Grade Students

Calendar Organizer

23

Standards-Based SOCIAL STUDIES Graphic Organizers,
Rubrics, and Writing Prompts for Middle Grade Students

Build A Case

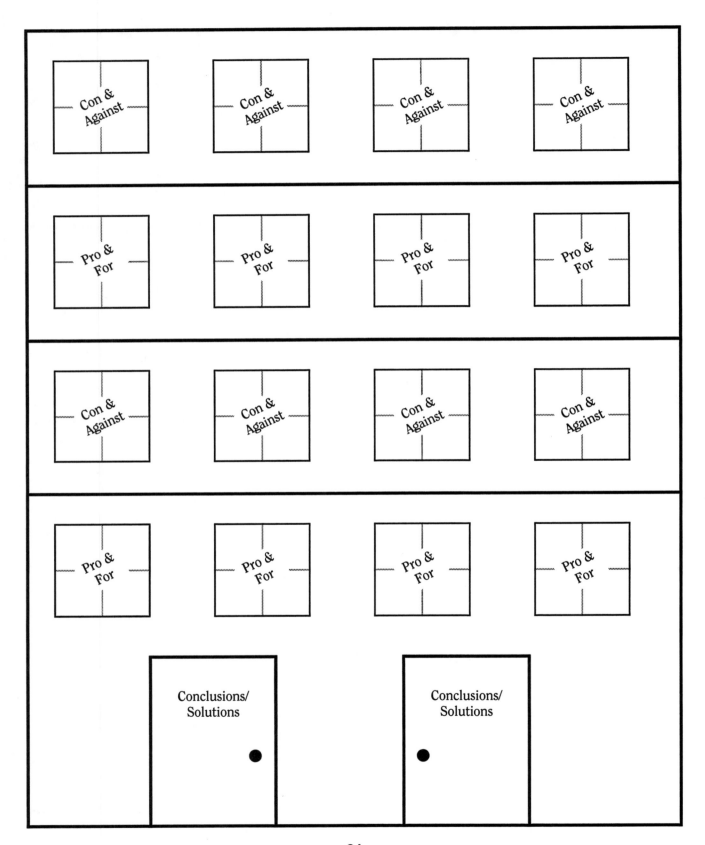

Con & Against

Con & Against

Con & Against

Con & Against

Pro & For

Pro & For

Pro & For

Pro & For

Con & Against

Con & Against

Con & Against

Con & Against

Pro & For

Pro & For

Pro & For

Pro & For

Conclusions/ Solutions

Conclusions/ Solutions

Standards-Based SOCIAL STUDIES Graphic Organizers,
Rubrics, and Writing Prompts for Middle Grade Students

Concept Map

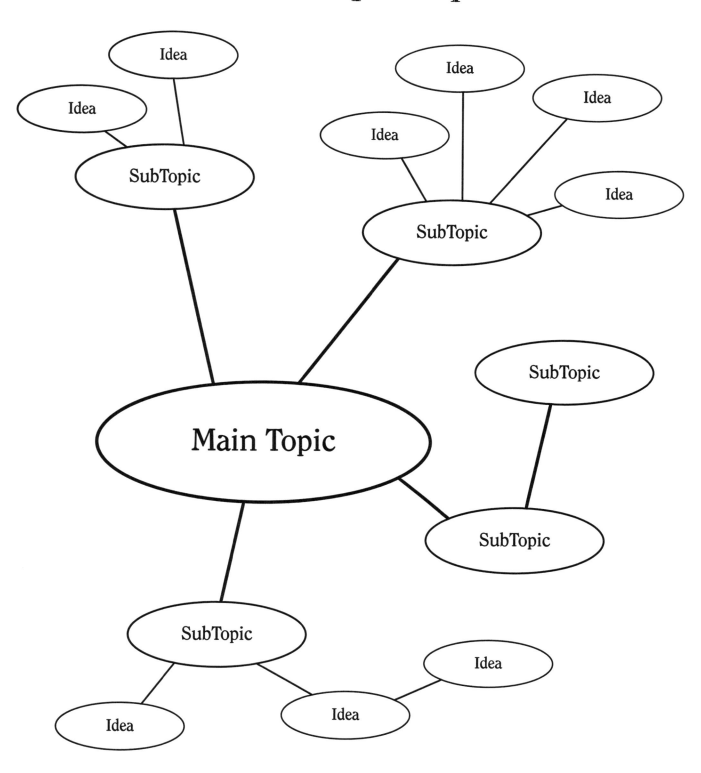

Standards-Based SOCIAL STUDIES Graphic Organizers,
Rubrics, and Writing Prompts for Middle Grade Students

Cultural Heroes

My List Of Heroes	My List Of Decision-Makers	My List Of Victims	My List Of Leaders
My List Of Facilitators	My List Of Conformists	My List Of Troublemakers	My List Of Pacifists

26

Data Graph

Data Graph Topic	Data Graph Summary

Standards-Based SOCIAL STUDIES Graphic Organizers,
Rubrics, and Writing Prompts for Middle Grade Students

Decision-Making Chart

Optional Positions / Outcomes	Criteria To Consider					Rating
1.						
2.						
3.						
4.						
5.						
6.						
Comments						

Event-Tracking Map

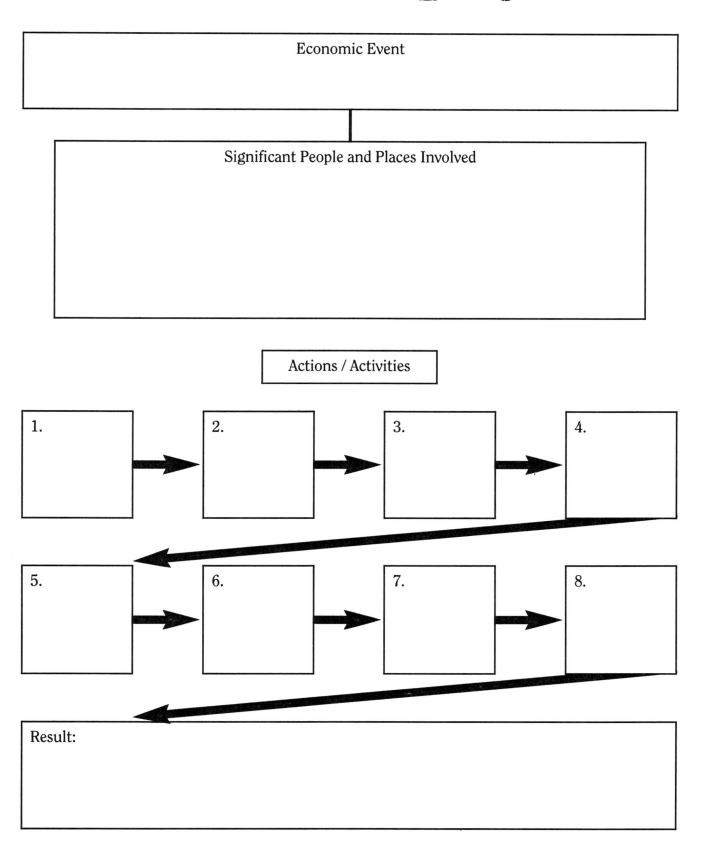

Economic Event

Significant People and Places Involved

Actions / Activities

1.

2.

3.

4.

5.

6.

7.

8.

Result:

Standards-Based SOCIAL STUDIES Graphic Organizers,
Rubrics, and Writing Prompts for Middle Grade Students

Famous Person Chart

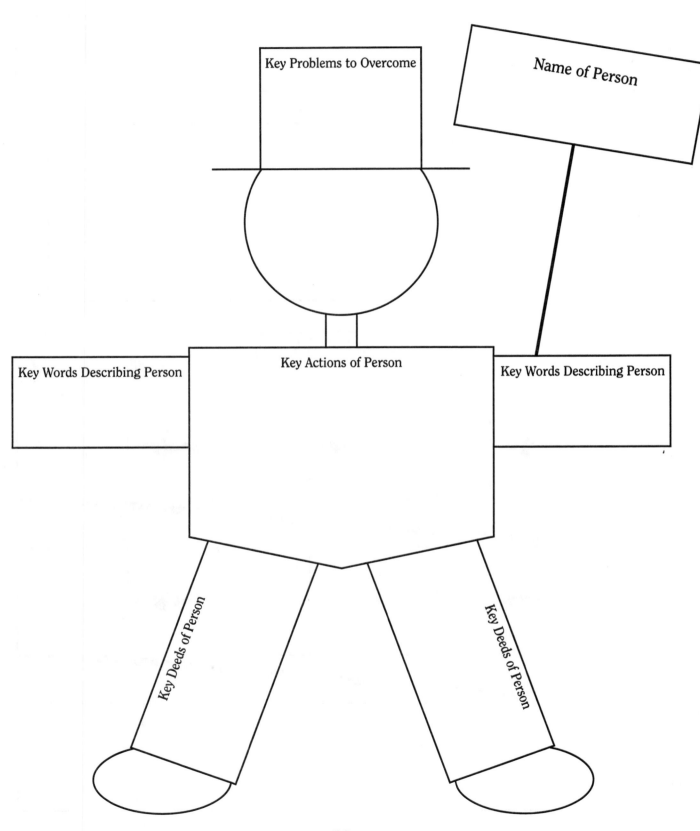

Key Problems to Overcome

Name of Person

Key Words Describing Person

Key Actions of Person

Key Words Describing Person

Key Deeds of Person

Key Deeds of Person

Standards-Based SOCIAL STUDIES Graphic Organizers,
Rubrics, and Writing Prompts for Middle Grade Students

Interdisciplinary Tree

SOCIAL STUDIES

ART

SCIENCE

MUSIC

LANGUAGE

MATH

*Standards-Based SOCIAL STUDIES Graphic Organizers,
Rubrics, and Writing Prompts for Middle Grade Students*

Interview Organizer

GETTING READY FOR THE INTERVIEW

Name of Interviewee _____

Name of Interviewer _____

Date of Interview _____

Purpose of Interview _____

_____

CONDUCTING THE INTERVIEW

Question One _____

_____

Response _____

_____

Question Two _____

_____

Response _____

_____

Question Three _____

_____

Response _____

_____

FOLLOWING THE INTERVIEW

Results of Interview _____

_____

_____

_____

_____

Standards-Based SOCIAL STUDIES Graphic Organizers, Rubrics, and Writing Prompts for Middle Grade Students

KWL Chart

Topic of Study_____

Student's Name _____

K What I Know	W What I Want to Know	L What I Learned

Standards-Based SOCIAL STUDIES Graphic Organizers,
Rubrics, and Writing Prompts for Middle Grade Students

Maps

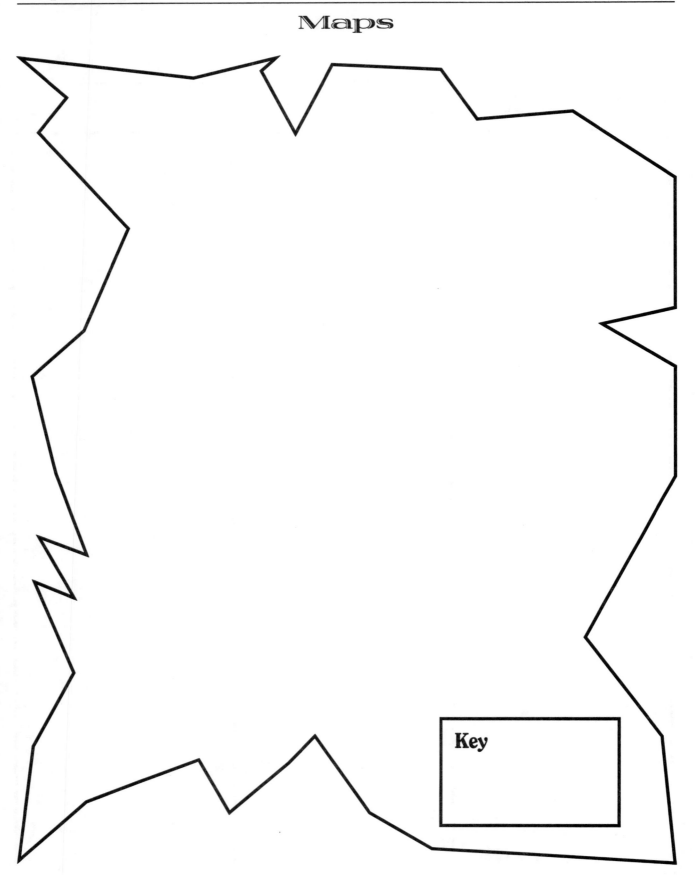

Key

Matrix

NAMES OF OBJECTS	Criterion	Criterion	Criterion	Criterion	Criterion	Criterion	Criterion	Criterion	Criterion	Criterion	Criterion	Criterion
1.												
2.												
3.												
4.												
5.												
6.												
7.												
8.												
9.												
10.												
11.												
12.												
13.												
14.												
15.												
16.												
17.												
18.												
19.												
20.												

Standards-Based SOCIAL STUDIES Graphic Organizers, Rubrics, and Writing Prompts for Middle Grade Students

Observation Log

Date: _____ Time: _____

Date: _____ Time: _____

Date: _____ Time: _____

Date: _____ Time: _____

Date: _____ Time: _____

Date: _____ Time: _____

Picture Puzzle

Topic _____

Student's Name _____

*Standards-Based SOCIAL STUDIES Graphic Organizers,
Rubrics, and Writing Prompts for Middle Grade Students*

Points to Ponder

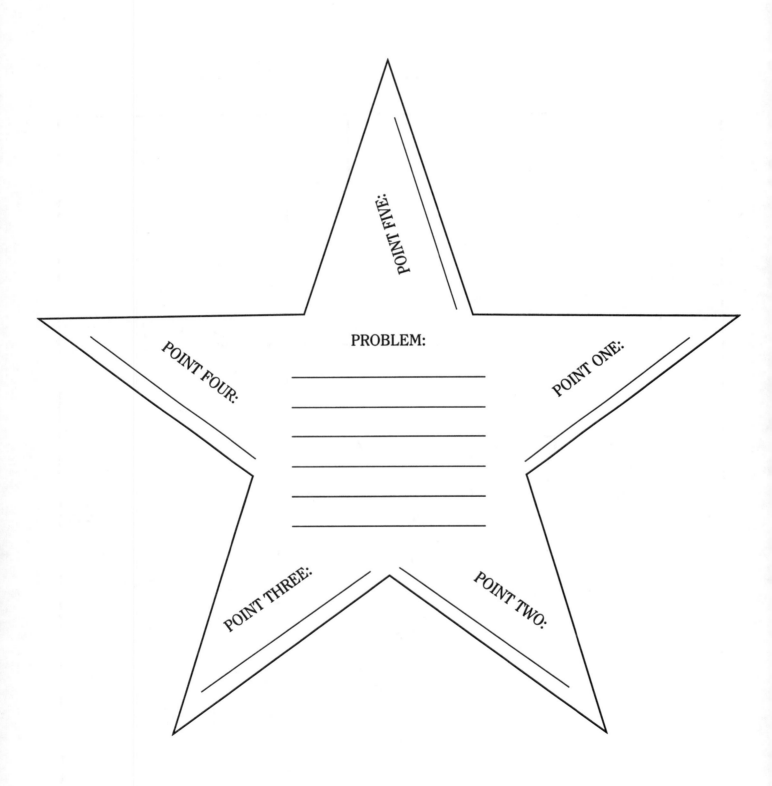

POINT FIVE:

PROBLEM:

POINT FOUR:

POINT ONE:

POINT THREE:

POINT TWO:

Read-to-Know Chart

	Section Title	What I Expect To Learn	What I Learned
1.			
2.			
3.			
4.			
5.			
6.			
7.			
8.			
9.			

*Standards-Based SOCIAL STUDIES Graphic Organizers,
Rubrics, and Writing Prompts for Middle Grade Students*

Scope and Sequence Map

Historical Setting	
Historical Figures	
Historical Problem Situation	

First Event/Step: _____

Second Event/Step: _____

Third Event/Step: _____

Fourth Event/Step: _____

Fifth Event/Step: _____

Outcomes: _____
_____

Resolution: _____
_____

Story Board

1.	6.
2.	7.
3.	8.
4.	9.
5.	10.

Standards-Based SOCIAL STUDIES Graphic Organizers,
Rubrics, and Writing Prompts for Middle Grade Students

Graphic Organizer

What, So What, Now What?

Topic of Study_____

Student's Name _____

What?	So What?	And Now What?

Standards-Based SOCIAL STUDIES Graphic Organizers,
Rubrics, and Writing Prompts for Middle Grade Students

42

Copyright ©2001 by Incentive Publications, Inc.
Nashville, TN.

Venn Diagram

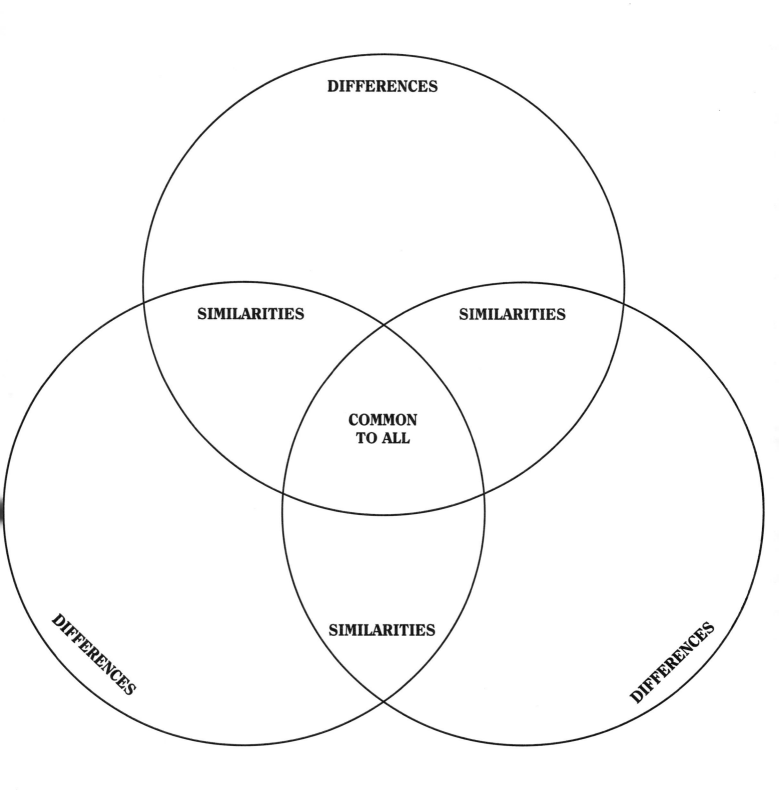

*Standards-Based SOCIAL STUDIES Graphic Organizers,
Rubrics, and Writing Prompts for Middle Grade Students*

Questions for Teachers and Students to Consider About Using Graphic Organizers in the Classroom

1. What is a graphic organizer and what types of graphic organizers are best for my subject area?

2. How can I use graphic organizers to help students collect information, make interpretations, draw conclusions, solve problems, outline plans, and become better reflective thinkers?

3. What graphic organizers can I use that are hierarchical structures with levels and subsets?

4. What graphic organizers can I use that are conceptual structures which take a central idea or concept and branch out from it?

5. What graphic organizers can I use that are sequential structures that focus on the order, chronology, or flow of ideas?

6. What graphic organizers can I use that are cyclical structures, which form a pattern in a circular format?

7. How can I model the use of graphic organizers with my students before introducing them into the instructional process?

8. How can I best model the use of graphic organizers with a wall chart, an overhead projector, or a drawing on the chalkboard?

9. How do graphic organizers show and explain relationships between content and sub-content and how do they in turn relate to the other content areas?

10. How can graphic organizers be considered teaching tools for all types of learners?

11. How can graphic organizers be used as assessment tools to show a student's understanding of a concept and a student's way of thinking about that concept?

12. How do graphic organizers support Bloom's Taxonomy and the Multiple Intelligences?

13. Are graphic organizers best used with individual students or can they be part of cooperative learning group tasks?

14. How can students use graphic organizers to assess their own learning?

Standards-Based SOCIAL STUDIES Graphic Organizers, Rubrics, and Writing Prompts for Middle Grade Students

Writing Prompts

Discuss your cultural background or heritage.

_____
_____
_____
_____
_____
_____
_____

If you were to create a time capsule around the theme of science and technology depicting changes during the past decade, what items would you choose to put in it and why?

_____
_____
_____
_____
_____
_____
_____
_____
_____

Pick a controversial social issue and speculate as to how the following human factors might impact their views of that issue—political party, religious beliefs, lifestyle, age, gender, and occupation.

_____
_____
_____
_____
_____
_____
_____
_____

GUIDELINES
FOR USING WRITING PROMPTS

PURPOSE

How do you present the purposes of a journal to your students when you are making journal assignments? A journal is: a collection of ideas, thoughts, and opinions; a place to outline papers and projects, a place to record observations about something read, written or discussed, a record keeping tool, a place in which to write personal reactions or responses, a reference file to help a student monitor individual growth, a way for students to dialogue with teachers and peers, a place for a student to write about a variety of topics, and a place for reflections on learned material.

FORMATS

Several formats are available for students working with journal writing. Some of the most appealing formats to students and teachers are: special notebooks, segments of audiotapes, file cards, and handmade diaries.

WRITING TIME

There are several approaches students may use in timing their journal writing. Some may write daily for five minutes, semi-weekly for ten minutes, weekly for fifteen minutes, or write as inspiration strikes.

STUDENT FEEDBACK

There are several methods, both formal and informal, for sharing students' journal work. Choose one or more of the following to implement in your classroom.
1) Students share their journal entries with their peers.
2) Students read journal entries aloud to the class on a volunteer basis.
3) Journals may be used for "conferencing."
4) Journals are to be taken home and shared with parents or guardians.
5) Students may analyze and answer one of their own journal entries one or more days after entry was recorded to acknowledge personal changes in perspective.

Standards-Based SOCIAL STUDIES Graphic Organizers,
Rubrics, and Writing Prompts for Middle Grade Students

Copyright ©2001 by Incentive Publications, Inc.
Nashville, TN.

Write down as many different worldwide religions as you can think of and record at least one interesting fact or perception you have about each one. Then write down a question you would most like to ask someone practicing that belief.

_____

_____

_____

_____

_____

_____

_____

_____

_____

_____

_____

Define the word "culture" in your own words. What things make up a given culture? Do all cultures have the same basic needs? The same values? The same goals? How do you know?

_____

_____

_____

_____

_____

_____

_____

_____

_____

_____

_____

Imagine you are a famous producer of films. You have just been hired to create a documentary on the most unique or unusual culture in the world. What culture would you choose and what would you documentary be like?

_____

_____

_____

_____

_____

_____

_____

_____

_____

_____

Describe your favorite Chinese, Mexican, Italian, German, or Turkish food in mouth-watering terms. Create a newspaper ad to advertise a restaurant you think would be featuring this food as its "signature dish." Draw a picture to illustrate the ad.

_____

_____

_____

_____

_____

_____

_____

_____

_____

_____

Standards-Based SOCIAL STUDIES Graphic Organizers, Rubrics, and Writing Prompts for Middle Grade Students

Explain what you think is meant by the term "culture shock." Who is likely to experience culture shock? What can one do to avoid it or treat it?

_____

_____

_____

_____

_____

_____

_____

_____

_____

_____

Discuss your cultural background or heritage.

_____

_____

_____

_____

_____

_____

_____

_____

_____

_____

_____

Standards-Based SOCIAL STUDIES Graphic Organizers,
Rubrics, and Writing Prompts for Middle Grade Students

Mahatma Gandhi of India advocated political change and justice without violence. Cite a situation where this has been accomplished and a situation where violence continues to be a problem due to cultural differences.

_____

_____

_____

_____

_____

_____

_____

_____

_____

_____

The tea ceremony in Japan is an important part of Japanese culture and requires thoughtful preparation and serving of the tea. Describe a special ceremony that is popular in your culture today.

_____

_____

_____

_____

_____

_____

_____

_____

_____

_____

Standards-Based SOCIAL STUDIES Graphic Organizers, Rubrics, and Writing Prompts for Middle Grade Students

It has been said, "History repeats itself." Give examples where this has been true.

_____

_____

_____

_____

_____

_____

_____

_____

_____

_____

_____

_____

If you could go back in time to live during any historical period, which one would you choose and why? Which one would you avoid and why?

_____

_____

_____

_____

_____

_____

_____

_____

_____

_____

Standards-Based SOCIAL STUDIES Graphic Organizers,
Rubrics, and Writing Prompts for Middle Grade Students

Pretend you were present at an important historical event such as the Boston Tea Party, the bombing of Pearl Harbor, or the writing of the Declaration of Independence and describe what it was like.

_____

_____

_____

_____

_____

_____

_____

_____

_____

_____

Explain why you think the study of history is important to the education of an informed populace?

_____

_____

_____

_____

_____

_____

_____

_____

_____

Standards-Based SOCIAL STUDIES Graphic Organizers,
Rubrics, and Writing Prompts for Middle Grade Students

History is the recording of past events. Create a personal timeline depicting the key growth events in your own history up to this point in time.

_____

_____

_____

_____

_____

_____

_____

_____

_____

_____

Generate a list of ten different inventions that you think have had the most historical significance or impact on lifestyles since the early 1800s.

_____

_____

_____

_____

_____

_____

_____

_____

_____

_____

Standards-Based SOCIAL STUDIES Graphic Organizers,
Rubrics, and Writing Prompts for Middle Grade Students

Define *freedom* and describe how a government should work to protect the freedom of its people.

_____

_____

_____

_____

_____

_____

_____

_____

_____

_____

Would you want to be the king or queen of a country? Explain.

_____

_____

_____

_____

_____

_____

_____

_____

_____

_____

_____

What famous world leader do you most admire and why?

_____

_____

_____

_____

_____

_____

_____

_____

_____

_____

_____

What arguments would you make for living in a democracy (a government run by the people) over those living in an autocracy (government run by an individual)?

_____

_____

_____

_____

_____

_____

_____

_____

_____

_____

_____

Standards-Based SOCIAL STUDIES Graphic Organizers,
Rubrics, and Writing Prompts for Middle Grade Students

Discuss the three branches of government in America—legislative, judicial, and executive—as it relates to the concept of power.

_____

_____

_____

_____

_____

_____

_____

_____

_____

_____

Write about the ways that the government provides for the poor, the unemployed, the disabled, and the abused.

_____

_____

_____

_____

_____

_____

_____

_____

_____

_____

Standards-Based SOCIAL STUDIES Graphic Organizers,
Rubrics, and Writing Prompts for Middle Grade Students

Name as many different currencies as you can think of and predict which one has the greatest value when compared to the United States dollar. Explain why currency values fluctuate over time.

_____

_____

_____

_____

_____

_____

_____

_____

_____

_____

_____

Imagine that you are taking a hot air balloon ride over a thriving marketplace in a European or South American country. Write about what you see as you hang over the basket and watch the sights and sounds of people buying, bargaining, and selling things.

_____

_____

_____

_____

_____

_____

_____

_____

_____

_____

_____

Standards-Based SOCIAL STUDIES Graphic Organizers,
Rubrics, and Writing Prompts for Middle Grade Students

Write about what you think people should and should not do to invest wisely in the stock market.

_____

_____

_____

_____

_____

_____

_____

_____

_____

_____

_____

_____

_____

Pretend that you are going to open up a consignment or second-hand shop for kids. Describe how you will collect items to sell, how you will market them, and how you will recruit and satisfy your customers.

_____

_____

_____

_____

_____

_____

_____

_____

_____

_____

_____

_____

Standards-Based SOCIAL STUDIES Graphic Organizers,
Rubrics, and Writing Prompts for Middle Grade Students

Describe what part advertising plays in the world of consumer spending. What commercial ads most influence you? It has been said that advertising is legalized lying. Do you agree or disagree with this statement?

_____

_____

_____

_____

_____

_____

_____

_____

_____

Explain the concepts of "import" and "export" by discussing why a country exports things they produce and how they also determine what to import for themselves. Do you believe in "free trade" to promote this type of economic exchange between and among countries?

_____

_____

_____

_____

_____

_____

_____

_____

_____

_____

Standards-Based SOCIAL STUDIES Graphic Organizers,
Rubrics, and Writing Prompts for Middle Grade Students

Explain when you would choose a globe for getting information and when you think a map might be a better tool. Why is it important to have the imaginary grid of latitude and longitude represented on a globe or map?

_____

_____

_____

_____

_____

_____

_____

_____

_____

_____

Summarize how the geography and climate of an area can significantly influence various forms of shelter such as a log cabin, igloo, thatched hut, houseboat, or condominium.

_____

_____

_____

_____

_____

_____

_____

_____

_____

Standards-Based SOCIAL STUDIES Graphic Organizers,
Rubrics, and Writing Prompts for Middle Grade Students

William Wordsworth, a 19th century English poet, once wrote: "Nature never did betray the heart that loved her." In what ways, do humans betray nature today?

_____

_____

_____

_____

_____

_____

_____

_____

_____

_____

Agree or disagree with this statement: Geography is important to a civilization. Give examples to support your position.

_____

_____

_____

_____

_____

_____

_____

_____

_____

_____

_____

Standards-Based SOCIAL STUDIES Graphic Organizers,
Rubrics, and Writing Prompts for Middle Grade Students

Write about where in the world you would like to hike or bike.

_____

_____

_____

_____

_____

_____

_____

_____

_____

_____

_____

Compose a message you would like to send to an environmentalist.

_____

_____

_____

_____

_____

_____

_____

_____

_____

_____

_____

_____

List the five most important rights and responsibilities of a model citizen.

_____

_____

_____

_____

_____

_____

_____

_____

_____

_____

_____

John F. Kennedy was famous for saying, "Ask not what your country can do for you, but what you can do for your country." What things do you plan to do for your country as you grow older?

_____

_____

_____

_____

_____

_____

_____

_____

_____

_____

_____

Consider the death penalty from the position of a judge, a taxpayer, a criminal, a victim, and a prosecuting attorney.

_____

_____

_____

_____

_____

_____

_____

_____

_____

_____

Pick a controversial social issue and speculate as to how the following human factors might impact their views of that issue—political party, religious beliefs, lifestyle, age, gender, and occupation.

_____

_____

_____

_____

_____

_____

_____

_____

_____

_____

_____

Standards-Based SOCIAL STUDIES Graphic Organizers,
Rubrics, and Writing Prompts for Middle Grade Students

Give living examples of these ideals, principles, and practices of citizenship in a democratic republic-----liberty, justice, equality, and human dignity.

_____

_____

_____

_____

_____

_____

_____

_____

_____

_____

How do you and your family practice good citizenship at home, at school, and in your community?

_____

_____

_____

_____

_____

_____

_____

_____

_____

_____

_____

*Standards-Based SOCIAL STUDIES Graphic Organizers,
Rubrics, and Writing Prompts for Middle Grade Students*

Explain the relationship, if any, between patriotism and citizenship.

_____

_____

_____

_____

_____

_____

_____

_____

_____

_____

_____

_____

As a citizen, if you were asked to advise your government on whether to spend more money on education, the environment, national defense, health care, the poor, or space exploration, which one would you choose and why?

_____

_____

_____

_____

_____

_____

_____

_____

_____

_____

_____

Standards-Based SOCIAL STUDIES Graphic Organizers, Rubrics, and Writing Prompts for Middle Grade Students

If you could go back in time and have a conversation with any three people who are now deceased and ask them for advice, who would you choose and what would you want to know?

_____

_____

_____

_____

_____

_____

_____

_____

_____

_____

Who has it easier in this world-----boys or girls? Explain.

_____

_____

_____

_____

_____

_____

_____

_____

_____

_____

_____

What would you say or do to someone who cheated on a test, shoplifted in a store, took illegal drugs, or spread untrue rumors about others. What actions would you take?

_____

_____

_____

_____

_____

_____

_____

_____

_____

_____

Create a plan to become a healthier person physically, emotionally, intellectually, or socially.

_____

_____

_____

_____

_____

_____

_____

_____

_____

_____

_____

Standards-Based SOCIAL STUDIES Graphic Organizers,
Rubrics, and Writing Prompts for Middle Grade Students

Define "institution" and describe ways that various institutions work to meet individual needs and to promote the common good. Are there any institutions that fail to do so? Justify your answer.

_____

_____

_____

_____

_____

_____

_____

_____

_____

_____

What do you think future generations will learn about us from the remains of our existing government policies and laws?

_____

_____

_____

_____

_____

_____

_____

_____

_____

_____

_____

Standards-Based SOCIAL STUDIES Graphic Organizers,
Rubrics, and Writing Prompts for Middle Grade Students

Generate a list of groups that provide you with fun things to do in your life. How many of these cost money? How many of these are available to everybody including the poor, the homeless, the disabled, minority groups, or the uneducated?

_____

_____

_____

_____

_____

_____

_____

_____

_____

_____

Is there a rule in your home, school, or community that you think should be changed? Is there a rule in your home, school, or community that you think should be mandated? How would you feel about a rule that imposed a curfew on young people or a rule that took away a young person's driver's license if he/she failed a subject or became a truant? Discuss.

_____

_____

_____

_____

_____

_____

_____

_____

_____

Standards-Based SOCIAL STUDIES Graphic Organizers, Rubrics, and Writing Prompts for Middle Grade Students

If the United States Department of Labor reported to the American public today that people, including teenagers work too hard, how would you respond? Do you agree or disagree with this statement: "Play is the work of children." Explain.

_____

_____

_____

_____

_____

_____

_____

_____

_____

_____

What individual, group, or institution do you think is best preparing you and your loved ones for both continuity and change in this complex world. Give examples to support your position.

_____

_____

_____

_____

_____

_____

_____

_____

_____

_____

_____

What if you were not required by law to attend school? Outline a plan for becoming educated and informed about the world in which you live. Think about the concept of "home schooling." Develop a list of "standards" that could be used as a guide for developing a course of study for students at your grade level.

_____

_____

_____

_____

_____

_____

_____

_____

_____

"Latchkey children" are common in today's society because many kids must come home to an empty house after school due to the fact that both parents work. Describe what kids, parents, schools, and community institutions could do to ensure the safety of these young people.

_____

_____

_____

_____

_____

_____

_____

_____

_____

_____

Standards-Based SOCIAL STUDIES Graphic Organizers, Rubrics, and Writing Prompts for Middle Grade Students

Conclude how language, art, and music have facilitated global understanding over time. Then examine ways language, art, and music may have led to misunderstandings over time. Do you think that art and music have a universal appeal regardless of culture? Explain.

_____

_____

_____

_____

_____

_____

_____

_____

_____

_____

Vincent Van Gogh, the Dutch painter, once said: "I dream my painting, and then I paint my dream." What is your dream for the globalization of the world?

_____

_____

_____

_____

_____

_____

_____

_____

_____

_____

How does interdependence promote global connections? Give examples to clarify your position.

_____
_____
_____
_____
_____
_____
_____
_____
_____
_____
_____
_____
_____

Discuss ways that the media helps and hinders positive global awareness.

_____
_____
_____
_____
_____
_____
_____
_____
_____
_____
_____
_____
_____

Standards-Based SOCIAL STUDIES Graphic Organizers,
Rubrics, and Writing Prompts for Middle Grade Students

Copyright ©2001 by Incentive Publications, Inc.
Nashville, TN.

Describe one relationship or tension that exists worldwide between personal wants and needs. Consider imported oil, land use, or environmental protection efforts.

_____

_____

_____

_____

_____

_____

_____

_____

_____

_____

_____

Pretend that scientists from several countries, including the United States, China, and Africa, have decided to work together to build an international medical center for the research and treatment of AIDS. What problems might the scientists run into as a result of their different origins and cultures? What advantages might there be to these different perspectives?

_____

_____

_____

_____

_____

_____

_____

_____

_____

_____

_____

Standards-Based SOCIAL STUDIES Graphic Organizers,
Rubrics, and Writing Prompts for Middle Grade Students

A tariff is a tax on goods coming in or going out of a country. How do you think these tariffs should be determined and how should their revenues be spent. How can tariffs enhance or reduce effective global connections and interdependence?

_____

_____

_____

_____

_____

_____

_____

_____

_____

_____

_____

Discuss all the different ways that we have of finding out what is going on throughout the world and rank these in order from the easiest to the most difficult, from the slowest to the fastest, and from the most interesting to the least interesting. Is cost ever a factor?

_____

_____

_____

_____

_____

_____

_____

_____

_____

_____

_____

Standards-Based SOCIAL STUDIES Graphic Organizers,
Rubrics, and Writing Prompts for Middle Grade Students

Write down at least ten revolutionary discoveries, inventions, or innovations in either the field of transportation or the field of communication that did not exist 100 years ago. Organize these into a chart, graph, or outline form.

_____

_____

_____

_____

_____

_____

_____

_____

_____

_____

Think of some ways that science and technology have led to some unpleasant changes in our physical environment (air, water, land). Be specific in your examples and comments.

_____

_____

_____

_____

_____

_____

_____

_____

_____

_____

Standards-Based SOCIAL STUDIES Graphic Organizers,
Rubrics, and Writing Prompts for Middle Grade Students

Astronaut Neil Armstrong said as he walked on the moon, "That's one small step for man, one giant leap for mankind." Agree or disagree with his statement giving personal thoughts and ideas on the subject of space exploration.

_____

_____

_____

_____

_____

_____

_____

_____

_____

_____

_____

If you were to create a time capsule around the theme of science and technology depicting changes during the past decade, what items would you choose to put in it and why?

_____

_____

_____

_____

_____

_____

_____

_____

_____

_____

_____

Standards-Based SOCIAL STUDIES Graphic Organizers,
Rubrics, and Writing Prompts for Middle Grade Students
Copyright ©2001 by Incentive Publications, Inc.
Nashville, TN.

Discuss some of the "evils" of technology such as invasion of privacy, pornography, computer viruses, fraud, piracy, and plagiarism.

_____

_____

_____

_____

_____

_____

_____

_____

_____

_____

Do you think science and technology have a significant impact on a person's values, beliefs, and attitudes in any way? Explain.

_____

_____

_____

_____

_____

_____

_____

_____

_____

_____

1. How can I fit journals into my particular discipline and classroom schedule?

2. How do I know if journals will work with my students or my subject area?

3. How can I coordinate journals with my team members and their classes?

4. What materials will I need to begin the use of journals?

5. How will I introduce the concept of journals to my students?

6. What kinds of reactions and responses can I expect from my students in their journal entries?

7. How can I get a sense of ownership or interest by students with journal prompts in my classroom?

8. How will I find time to reply to their journals, and what kind of responses should I write?

9. How can I overcome student resistance or misunderstanding of the journal concept?

10. How can I use journals for assessment purposes, and what kinds of information am I likely to receive from them?

11. How should I review or evaluate journals, and how will I keep track of this process?

12. How do I grade journal entries?

Rubrics

Guidelines
for Understanding and Using Rubrics

1. Agree on a definition of a rubric and its importance to the evaluation process. The purpose of a rubric is to answer the question: "What are the conditions of success and to what degree are those conditions met by the student involved in a specific learning task?"

2. Effective rubrics reflect the most important elements of an assigned task, product, or performance and they enable both student and teacher to accurately depict the level of competence or stage of development of that student.

3. Effective rubrics encourage student self-evaluations and, in fact, are shared with students prior to beginning the task so that students know exactly what represents quality work.

4. Rubrics are designed to ex... and are less subjective tha...

5. Every rubric must have ... for quality work on a spe... proficiency or degrees of ...

6. A holistic rubric consists ... of proficiency has a para... specific level.

7. An analytic rubric cons... accompanied with the ... or under each criterio...

8. Before implementing ... the elements of a qua... rubrics as models for ...

Standards-Based Social Studies Graphic Organizers

Social Studies
Independent Project Checklist

	Yes	√	No
1. My topic was well selected and appropriate for an independent study. My thoughts, ideas, and information are presented in a logical, sequential manner.			
2. I have eliminated unnecessary, confusing, irrelevant, or redundant words or phrases from my work.			
3. I have used examples, illustrations, graphic organizers, and/or analogies to explain or clarify main ideas or important concepts.			
4. I have some unusual or extraordinary descriptive words or phrases and colorful language to add interest to my work.			
5. I have included necessary information and re... I have eliminated unnecessary or irrelevant f... make a report lively and relevant.			
6. I have included a good balance of different k... to maintain the reader's interest throughout...			
7. I have checked my spelling, grammar, and p... carefully.			
8. The culmination or conclusion of my proje... enough to leave my reader with a better un... subject, some new ideas, and thoughts to p...			
9. My writing is neat, clear, and easy to read.			
10. This project is representative of my absolu...			

Some things I would do differently if I were planning t...

_____

_____

Name _____

Project Topic _____

Copyright ©2002 by Incentive Publications, Inc. Nashville, TN. &5

Unit Performance Rubric
Different Forces Assessment Rubric

My Best Work   So-so   Not So Good

Draw the appropriate rating for your work in the unit next to each of the following statements.

1. I completed reading, research, and related assessments punctually and to the best of my ability. **Rating:** _____

2. I participated in group discussions and contributed some ideas of my own. **Rating:** _____

3. I used attentive listening skills during the discussions. **Rating:** _____

4. My worksheets and homework assignments were neat and well done. **Rating:** _____

5. I worked cooperatively with my classmates when we worked in groups. **Rating:** _____

6. My portfolio entry or summary report was interesting, and I think others would want to read it. **Rating:** _____

7. My understanding of the unit topic is thorough, and I have a good store of knowledge on which to base future study. **Rating:** _____

Comments by Student: _____

_____

_____

Signed _____ Date _____

Comments by Teacher: _____

_____

_____

Signed _____ Date _____

Copyright ©2002 by Incentive Publications, Inc. Nashville, TN.   103   *Standards-Based Social Studies Graphic Organizers*

Guidelines
FOR USING RUBRICS

1. Agree on a definition of a rubric and its importance to the evaluation process. The purpose of a rubric is to answer the question: "What are the conditions of success and to what degree are those conditions met by the student involved in a specific learning task?"

2. Effective rubrics reflect the most important elements of an assigned task, product, or performance and they enable both student and teacher to accurately depict the level of competence or stage of development of that student.

3. Effective rubrics encourage student self-evaluations and, in fact, are shared with students prior to beginning the task so that students know exactly what represents quality work.

4. Rubrics are designed to explain more concretely what a child knows and can do and are less subjective than other means of student evaluation.

5. Every rubric must have two components which are: (1) characteristics or criteria for quality work on a specific task and (2) determination of the specific levels of proficiency or degrees of success for each part of a task.

6. A holistic rubric consists of paragraphs arranged in a hierarchy so that each level of proficiency has a paragraph describing factors that would result in that specific level.

7. An analytic rubric consists of a listing of criteria most characteristic of that task accompanied with the degrees of success for each model listed separately beside or under each criterion.

8. Before implementing rubrics in a discipline, it is important to define and discuss the elements of a quality performance in that discipline and to collect samples of rubrics as models for scrutiny and potential application.

Standards-Based SOCIAL STUDIES Graphic Organizers,
Rubrics, and Writing Prompts for Middle Grade Students

9. Before implementing rubrics in a discipline, study samples of student work to determine realistic attributes common to varied performances at different levels of proficiency. Translate these attributes into descriptors for the degrees of proficiency and then establish a rating scale to delineate those degrees of proficiency.

10. Avoid using generalities such as *good, better, little, none,* or *somewhat* in your rating scales; quantify and qualify in more specific terms. Construct analytical rubrics with four to six degrees of proficiency for each criterion. Then, weight each criterion to determine the percentage or number of points each is worth.

11. Distribute and discuss any rubric directly with the student before he or she embarks on the assigned product or performance task. Encourage the student to set personal goals for their desired level of accomplishment on each criterion. Insist that students revise their work if it does not meet minimum expectations on any criterion of the task.

12. When introducing rubrics to students, start out by collaboratively constructing a rubric for a fun class event such as planning a party, structuring a field trip, or designing a contest.

13. Remember that to be most effective as an important component of social studies programs, rubrics must be accompanied by carefully planned opportunities for meta-cognitive reflections throughout the assessment experience. While rubrics are comprised of checklists containing sets of criteria for measuring the elements of product, performance, or portfolio, the meta-cognitive reflections provide for self-assessment observations completely unique to the students' own learning goals, expectations, and experiences.

14. The use of rubrics can augment, reinforce, personalize, and strengthen but not replace the assessment program mandated by curriculum guidelines or system requirements. As with any well-balanced assessment program the mastery teacher or teaching team will continue to take full advantage of all tools, strategies, and techniques available to construct and make use of a balanced assessment program to meet individual needs.

Artifact Show and Tell Assessment

Rating Scale: **I Great Show**   **II Good Show**   **III Poor Show**

---

1. Quality of Report Format   **Rating:** _____
Oral presentation uses artifacts related to the topic, with tags or file cards for each artifact explaining its significance, and decorated bag.

2. Quality of Information   **Rating:** _____
Oral presentation is well researched and artifacts are very relevant to information on topic.

3. Grammar   **Rating:** _____
Grammar of presentation and grammar and spelling of tags or file cards is correct.

4. Interest   **Rating:** _____
Artifacts and oral presentation are smoothly presented, interesting, clear, and informative.

5. Graphics/Creativity   **Rating:** _____
Artifacts are creatively chosen and ordered to convey topic information.

6. Choice of Presentation   **Rating:** _____
Upon reflection, an artifact show and tell presentation was the best way to present this report.

Comments by Student: _____

_____

_____

_____

Signed _____ Date _____

Comments by Teacher: _____

_____

_____

_____

Signed _____ Date _____

Diorama Report Assessment

Rating Scale:

First Place = Excellent	Second Place = Good	Third Place = Fair	Fourth Place = Poor

1. Quality of Format   Rating: _____
The diorama conveys information on my topic
in an interesting and thought-provoking manner.

2. Quality of Information   Rating: _____
My topic was well-researched, and the diorama conveys
a large amount of correct information that is important to the subject.

3. Vocabulary   Rating: _____
The vocabulary utilized for headings or descriptive materials is carefully selected and
properly used to provoke and maintain an interest and to convey important information.

4. Interest   Rating: _____
The diorama is attractive, engaging, and entertaining.

5. Graphics/Creativity   Rating: _____
The graphics, images, design, use of color, and layout of my diorama are of high quality.

Comments by Student: _____

_____

_____

_____

Signed _____ Date _____

Comments by Teacher: _____

_____

_____

_____

Signed _____ Date _____

*Standards-Based SOCIAL STUDIES Graphic Organizers,
Rubrics, and Writing Prompts for Middle Grade Students*

Game Report Assessment

Rating Scale: **1** Great Game   **2** Good Game   **3** Poor Showing

---

1. Quality of Report Format   Rating: _____
My report is a game that allows those who play it to learn about my topic.

2. Rules of Playing the Game   Rating: _____
Rules for playing the game are clear and concise and will be easily understood by the players.

3. Quality of Information   Rating: _____
My game conveys well-researched, key information on my topic.

4. Grammar   Rating: _____
Any text on my game shows perfect grammar and spelling.

5. Interest   Rating: _____
My game presents the information in an attractive and entertaining way that will hold the players' attention.

6. Graphics/Creativity   Rating: _____
My game uses the elements of my chosen game format creatively and effectively.

Comments by Student: _____

_____

_____

_____

Signed _____ Date _____

Comments by Teacher: _____

_____

_____

_____

Signed _____ Date _____

STUDENT CHECKLIST FOR CREATING A GROUP PROJECT

	Little Progress 1	2	Some Progress 3	4	Great Progress 5

1. I understood the nature of the assignment.
2. I had a role to play in completing the task.
3. I adhered to the rules.
4. I made meaningful contributions to the group in achieving group goals.
5. I worked cooperatively and responsibly with members of the group.
6. I practiced active listening skills with group members.
7. I displayed positive and constructive social skills.
8. I assumed responsibility for my actions.
9. I helped to motivate and energize the group to complete tasks.
10. I helped the group plan and implement its activities.

My major contribution to the group's effort was: _____

_____

Something I could do better next time is: _____

_____

Some comments from other members of the group about my performance are: _____

_____

Questions or remarks for my student/teacher conference: _____

_____

Standards-Based SOCIAL STUDIES Graphic Organizers, Rubrics, and Writing Prompts for Middle Grade Students

Portfolio Assessment

Rating Scale:

	1	2	3
	OK	Good	Terrific

Grading Scale
25–30 points = A
20–24 points = B
14–19 points = C
8–13 points = D
Under 8 points = Unacceptable

1. Appropriateness of topic selected

2. Variety and quality of research materials used

3. Organization and completeness of portfolio

4. Quality of artifacts collected

5. Creativity shown in work

6. Correctness of work (grammar, spelling, sentence structure, neatness, punctuation, etc.)

7. Evidence of learning concepts and/or applying skills

8. Reflection process

9. Evidence of enthusiasm and interest in assignments

10. Presentation of portfolio

Comments by Student: _____

_____

_____

Signed _____ Date _____

Comments by Teacher: _____

_____

_____

Signed _____ Date _____

Standards-Based SOCIAL STUDIES Graphic Organizers,
Rubrics, and Writing Prompts for Middle Grade Students

Journal Assessment

Rating Scale:

4	3	2	1
Slow Down	**Keep Going**	**Right On**	**WOW**

1. Quality of Report Format

Rating: _____

My journal report records dated entries about my topic including important events, activities, feelings, reactions to information, observations, experiences, summaries, and conclusions.

2. Quality of Information

Rating: _____

My journal is well researched and conveys important and accurate information on my topic.

3. Details and Descriptions

Rating: _____

I have used colorful vocabulary and original thought to present details and descriptions in a lively manner.

4. Grammar

Rating: _____

There are no errors in the grammar and spelling of my report.

5. Interest

Rating: _____

My report is interesting to read and holds the reader's attention.

6. Graphics/Creativity

Rating: _____

The information in my report is creatively organized and presented.

Comments by Student: _____

_____

_____

_____

Signed _____ Date _____

Comments by Teacher: _____

_____

_____

_____

Signed _____ Date _____

Matrix Assessment

Rating Scale:

1	**2**	**3**
Best	**Next Best**	**Keep Working**

1. Quality of Report Format
Rating: _____

The Matrix Report includes appropriate categories and information in rows and columns.

2. Quality of Information
Rating: _____

The information in my report demonstrates significant research into the topic.

3. Grammar
Rating: _____

There are no spelling or grammar errors in my report.

4. Interest
Rating: _____

The different elements and comparative features in my matrix highlight the main points of my topic and explain the topic well.

5. Graphics/Creativity
Rating: _____

The layout and selection of information is creative and original.

Comments by Student: _____

_____

_____

_____

_____

Signed _____ Date _____

Comments by Teacher: _____

_____

_____

_____

_____

Signed _____ Date _____

Mural Report Assessment

Rating Scale:

1 First Place	**2** Second Place	**3** Third Place

---

1. Quality of Report Format
Rating: _____

Our mural report is made of one mural divided into sections, one section for each group member. Each section uses text and graphics to illustrate a portion of the topic.

---

2. Quality of Information
Rating: _____

The information in our mural is organized in a logical sequence and is presented well to convey information on our topic.

---

3. Grammar
Rating: _____

Our mural report contains no grammar or spelling errors.

---

4. Interest
Rating: _____

Our report using the mural format makes our topic easier to understand and more interesting to learn.

---

5. Graphics/Creativity
Rating: _____

Our mural is attractive and creative.

Comments by Student: _____

_____

_____

_____

Signed _____ Date _____

Comments by Teacher: _____

_____

_____

_____

Signed _____ Date _____

Newspaper Format Assessment

Rating Scale:

1	2	3
Star Reporter	**Desk Reporter**	**Cub Reporter**

1. Quality of Report Format   Rating: _____

My Newspaper Report includes a banner headline, columns, and different newspaper sections.

2. Quality of Information   Rating: _____

The information in my report demonstrates thorough research into my topic using a variety of resources.

3. Grammar   Rating: _____

There are no grammar or spelling errors in my Newspaper Report and it is neatly written.

4. Interest   Rating: _____

The different sections of my Newspaper Report present the main points of my topic and explain them well.

5. Graphics/Creativity   Rating: _____

The newspaper layout and illustrations are attractive and help convey information on my topic.

6. Coverage of Topic   Rating: _____

My topic is presented in a complete and concise manner to give the reader a good understanding of the subject.

Comments by Student: _____

_____

_____

Signed _____ Date _____

Comments by Teacher: _____

_____

_____

_____

Signed _____ Date _____

Standards-Based SOCIAL STUDIES Graphic Organizers, Rubrics, and Writing Prompts for Middle Grade Students

Research Project Assessment

		Best	Better	Good	Fair	Poor
1. Quality of Project Format My research project is composed of a series of notebook or file card entries presenting my assigned topic with each properly dated and sourced.		1	2	3	4	5
2. Quality of Information My notes show significant research, using a variety of resources.		1	2	3	4	5
3. Quality of Documentation My sources are fully and properly documented including complete bibliographical information.		1	2	3	4	5
4. Grammar I checked my work carefully and it is free of spelling and grammar errors.		1	2	3	4	5
5. Interest The items in my research project are diverse and appropriate for presenting key information and/or special highlights of the topic.		1	2	3	4	5
6. Graphics/Creativity The design, layout, and graphics/illustrations are creative and effective.		1	2	3	4	5

Comments by Student: _____

_____

_____

_____

Signed _____ Date _____

Comments by Teacher: _____

_____

_____

_____

Signed _____ Date _____

Standards-Based SOCIAL STUDIES Graphic Organizers, Rubrics, and Writing Prompts for Middle Grade Students

Report Assessment

Rating Scale:	Poor 4	Fair 3	Good 2	Great 1

---

1. Quality of Report Format   Rating: _____

The report presents relevant topic information neatly written or typed.

---

2. Quality of Information   Rating: _____

Important information is clearly conveyed.

---

3. Grammar   Rating: _____

The report's grammar and spelling is correct.

---

4. Details and Descriptions   Rating: _____

The report is attractive and interesting.
It presents details and descriptions important to the topic.

---

5. Graphics/Creativity   Rating: _____

The report is well organized in an original and creative manner.

Comments by Student: _____

_____

_____

_____

_____

Signed _____ Date _____

Comments by Teacher: _____

_____

_____

_____

_____

Signed _____ Date _____

Standards-Based SOCIAL STUDIES Graphic Organizers,
Rubrics, and Writing Prompts for Middle Grade Students

Social Studies
Independent Project Checklist

	Yes	√	No
1. My topic was well selected and appropriate for an independent study. My thoughts, ideas, and information are presented in a logical, sequential manner.			
2. I have eliminated unnecessary, confusing, irrelevant, or redundant words or phrases from my work.			
3. I have used examples, illustrations, graphic organizers, and/or analogies to explain or clarify main ideas or important concepts.			
4. I have some unusual or extraordinary descriptive words or phrases and colorful language to add interest to my work.			
5. I have included necessary information and related details and I have eliminated unnecessary or irrelevant facts in order to make a report lively and relevant.			
6. I have included a good balance of different kinds of sentences to maintain the reader's interest throughout my work.			
7. I have checked my spelling, grammar, and punctuation carefully.			
8. The culmination or conclusion of my project is interesting enough to leave my reader with a better understanding of my subject, some new ideas, and thoughts to ponder.			
9. My writing is neat, clear, and easy to read.			
10. This project is representative of my absolute best work.			

Some things I would do differently if I were planning this project (or a similar project) again are:

_____

_____

_____

Name _____ Date _____

Project Topic _____

Standards-Based SOCIAL STUDIES Graphic Organizers, Rubrics, and Writing Prompts for Middle Grade Students

Student Project or Assignment Reflection

Title: _____

1. Brief description of project:

   _____
   _____
   _____
   _____
   _____
   _____

2. Major objectives:

   _____
   _____
   _____

3. Resources used:

   _____
   _____
   _____

4. Major concepts learned from completion of project:

   _____
   _____
   _____

5. Main facts learned:

   _____
   _____
   _____

6. Skills used during completion of the project:

   _____
   _____

Standards-Based SOCIAL STUDIES Graphic Organizers,
Rubrics, and Writing Prompts for Middle Grade Students

7. New words added to my vocabulary through completion of the project:

_____

_____

_____

8. The most difficult part of the project was:

_____

_____

_____

9. The most interesting part of the project was:

_____

_____

_____

10. The thing I liked best about the project was:

_____

_____

_____

11. Meaningfulness of project
    (a) Extremely meaningful   (b) Somewhat meaningful   (c) Not very meaningful

12. If I were doing this project again I would . . .

_____

_____

_____

13. When I reflect on the requirement for this project and how I completed it, I would
    summarize my findings about how I did, what I learned, and its value to me as . . .

_____

_____

_____

14. The grade I feel I deserve for this project is:

_____

_____

_____

Student signature _____ Date _____

*Standards-Based SOCIAL STUDIES Graphic Organizers,
Rubrics, and Writing Prompts for Middle Grade Students*

STUDENT CHECKLIST FOR TECHNOLOGY PROJECT

NAME_____ DATE _____

	My Best Work A	Good Work B	I could have done better. C
1. I thought of several options for my technology project and discussed these with others.			
2. I selected a topic based on my interest, conversations with others, and available material on my topic.			
3. I created an outline for researching my topic.			
4. I researched my topic using the Internet and took notes on my findings.			
5. I cited various websites in my bibliography.			
6. I mastered the technical component of my project.			
7. I decided on a format appropriate for recording and reporting my information from the Internet.			
8. My comments and information in the project stem from my findings.			
9. I have incorporated creativity in my project.			
10. I have proofread my writing to check for spelling and grammar errors.			

If I were the teacher I would give this report a grade of *(circle 1)*   A   B   C   because . . .

_____

_____

Student Signature: _____

I am giving this report a grade of   A   B   C   because . . .

_____

_____

Teacher Signature: _____

Standards-Based SOCIAL STUDIES Graphic Organizers, Rubrics, and Writing Prompts for Middle Grade Students

Student/Teacher Evaluation

Name _____ Date Due_____

Topic

_____

Rating Scale

	√- needs more work	√ OK, not great	√+ Satisfactory	√++ Excellent

	Student	Teacher
Project requirement met		
Adequate research completed		
Project well organized		
Knowledge of topic sufficient		
Creative presentation of information		
Complete coverage of topic		
"Big Ideas" readily evident		
Details presented in an interesting way		
Punctuation, spelling, and grammar correct		
Clear and concise writing style		
Overall rating		

The strongest feature of the project is:

Student _____

Teacher _____

The weakest feature of the project is:

Student _____

Teacher _____

Recommendation for improvement:

Student _____

Teacher _____

Teacher Signature _____ Date _____

Standards-Based SOCIAL STUDIES Graphic Organizers,
Rubrics, and Writing Prompts for Middle Grade Students

Text Comprehension Rating Scale

Name of textbook: _____

Subject: _____

Page _____ to page _____

Great Understanding: 100–90

* Can answer questions asked about the text

* Can provide clear and explicit details about the text

* Can supply creative and insightful comments about the text

Good Understanding: 89–80

* Can discuss the text in chronological order and verbalize the highlights

* Can answer most questions asked about the text

* Can provide and discuss details about the text

* Can exhibit understanding of the text's content and intent

Poor Understanding: 79–0

* Have difficulty discussing the text and/or organizing facts in chronological order

* Can supply few details about the material read

* Have fuzzy answers and/or inconsistent answers to questions asked about the text

* Have difficulty verbalizing insights and/or personal reflections related to the text

---

Student Signature: _____ Date: _____

Teacher Signature: _____ Date: _____

Timeline Assessment

Rating Scale: Needs More Work: Ready   Fair: Set   Great: Go

1. Quality of Report Format
Rating: _____

My timeline includes an adequate number of benchmarks, with dates, paragraph descriptions of events/tasks, and graphics for each one organized according to date.

2. Quality of Information
Rating: _____

The data in my timeline is researched well and presented in a logical way.

3. Grammar
Rating: _____

My timeline report contains no grammar or spelling errors.

4. Interest
Rating: _____

My timeline makes my topic easier to understand and interesting to read.

5. Graphics/Creativity
Rating: _____

My timeline report uses the format creatively.

6. Choice of Format
Rating: _____

A timeline was the best way to present this material in a logical and sequenced manner.

Comments by Student: _____

_____

_____

_____

Signed _____ Date _____

Comments by Teacher: _____

_____

_____

_____

Signed _____ Date _____

Standards-Based SOCIAL STUDIES Graphic Organizers, Rubrics, and Writing Prompts for Middle Grade Students

Topic Collage Assessment

Rating Scale:

	First Place: Excellent	Second Place: Good	Third Place: Fair	Fourth Place: Poor

1. Quality of Report Format   Rating: _____

The collage conveys information on my topic in an interesting and thought-provoking manner.

2. Quality of Information   Rating: _____

My topic was well researched and the collage conveys a large amount of correct information important to the subject.

3. Content Selection   Rating: _____

All pictures and illustrations were carefully selected to present ideas and information concisely and in proper sequence.

4. Interest   Rating: _____

The collage is attractive and entertaining.

5. Graphics/Creativity   Rating: _____

The graphics, images, design, use of color, and layout of my collage are of high quality.

Comments by Student: _____

_____

_____

_____

Signed _____ Date _____

Comments by Teacher: _____

_____

_____

_____

Signed _____ Date _____

Standards-Based SOCIAL STUDIES Graphic Organizers, Rubrics, and Writing Prompts for Middle Grade Students

Unit Performance Rubric

My Best Work   **So-so**   **Not So Good**

Draw the appropriate rating for your work in the unit next to each of the following statements.

1. I completed reading, research, and related assessments punctually and to the best of my ability.   **Rating:** _____

2. I participated in group discussions and contributed some ideas of my own.   **Rating:** _____

3. I used attentive listening skills during the discussions.   **Rating:** _____

4. My worksheets and homework assignments were neat and well done. **Rating:** _____

5. I worked cooperatively with my classmates when we worked in groups. **Rating:** _____

6. My portfolio entry or summary report was interesting, and I think others would want to read it.   **Rating:** _____

7. My understanding of the unit topic is thorough, and I have a good store of knowledge on which to base future study.   **Rating:** _____

Comments by Student: _____

_____

_____

_____

Signed _____ Date _____

Comments by Teacher: _____

_____

_____

_____

Signed _____ Date _____

*Standards-Based SOCIAL STUDIES Graphic Organizers,
Rubrics, and Writing Prompts for Middle Grade Students*

Unit Vocabulary Check-Up

★ **Can recognize key words**
★★ **Can recognize and pronounce key words**
★★★ **Can recognize, pronounce, and tell the meaning of key words and terms**
★★★★ **Can use key words and terms in meaningful conversation or original writing.**

1. Vocabulary Words:

    1. _____   11. _____
    2. _____   12. _____
    3. _____   13. _____
    4. _____   14. _____
    5. _____   15. _____
    6. _____   16. _____
    7. _____   17. _____
    8. _____   18. _____
    9. _____   19. _____
   10. _____   20. _____

2. Six important words or terms that I know and can use related to the unit theme, but not on the above list, are:

    1. _____   4. _____
    2. _____   5. _____
    3. _____   6. _____

3. My understanding and independent use of the words and terms associated with this unit is:
   Fine   OK   Not so good   *(Circle one)*

Comments by Student: _____

_____

_____

_____

Signed _____ Date _____

Comments by Teacher: _____

_____

_____

_____

Signed _____ Date _____

Standards-Based SOCIAL STUDIES Graphic Organizers,
Rubrics, and Writing Prompts for Middle Grade Students

Visual Aid Assessment

Rating Scale	Best of Show I	Good Show II	Fair Show III	Poor Show IV

---

1. Quality of Presentation Format
Rating: _____

Oral presentation uses visual aids related to the presentation and of high interest.

---

2. Quality of Information
Rating: _____

Oral presentation is well researched and visual aids enhance and support the information presented.

---

3. Grammar
Rating: _____

Grammar and pronunciation of oral presentation and grammar and spelling of identification and/or descriptive tags or labels for visual aids is correct.

---

4. Interest
Rating: _____

Visual aids and oral presentation are well integrated, smoothly presented, interesting, clear, and informative.

---

5. Graphics/Creativity
Rating: _____

Visual aids are creatively chosen, ordered, and presented to convey topic information and add interest to the presentation.

---

6. Reflection
Rating: _____

Upon reflection, the visual aids used for this presentation were the best aids I could have used to hold my audience's attention and to convey the facts and information in a meaningful

way.

Comments by Student: _____

_____

_____

Signed _____ Date _____

Comments by Teacher: _____

_____

_____

Standards-Based SOCIAL STUDIES Graphic Organizers,
Rubrics, and Writing Prompts for Middle Grade Students

Student Assessment of Rubrics
As A Means of Measuring Student
Progress and/or as an Option for
More Traditional Assessment Tools

Directions: Circle one ([are] or [are not]) in statements 1–7 below and 9 on page 107:

1. I think rubrics [are] or [are not] a good tool for assessment because:

   _____

   _____

2. I think letter grades such as A B C D F [are] or [are not] a fair way to assess the quality of a Social Studies performance based task because:

   _____

   _____

3. In my opinion, multiple choice tests [are] or [are not] a good assessment tool for Social Studies programs because:

   _____

   _____

4. In my opinion, teacher made tests [are] or [are not] a good assessment tool for Social Studies programs because:

   _____

   _____

5. In my opinion, standardized tests [are] or [are not] a good assessment tool for Social Studies programs because:

   _____

   _____

6. In my opinion, essay type tests [are] or [are not] a good assessment tool for Social Studies programs because:

   _____

   _____

7. In my opinion, true/false tests [are] or [are not] a good assessment tool for Social Studies programs because:

   _____

   _____

8. If given a choice between teacher-made, true/false tests, essay type questions, multiple choice tests, or rubrics as an assessment to determine my social studies grade, I would choose

   _____ because:

   _____

   _____

9. I think the teacher comments [are] or [are not] an important part of rubric assessment form because:

_____

_____

10. I think my parents [understand] or [do not understand] (Circle one) the use of rubrics as an assessment tool and view them as [important] or [not important] (Circle one) in gaining a better understanding of my progress in Social Studies.

11. I think rubrics help me to communicate [more effectively] or [less effectively] (Circle one) with my teacher and, therefore, to measure my own progress in Social Studies [more] or [less] (circle one) than do traditional pencil and paper quizzes or end of chapter test questions.

12. The strengths and weaknesses of rubrics as a quantitative measure of my progress in Social Studies as I see them are:

Strengths: _____

_____

_____

Weaknesses: _____

_____

_____

On the whole, I would rate their value as an assessment tool as currently used in our social studies program as: (Circle One)

Extremely Valuable: Meaning and intent is clear, provides pertinent information for planning further study, and points out strengths and weaknesses of my work

Somewhat Valuable: Provides some insights to my progress and grasp of the knowledge and concepts studied, helps me to evaluate my performance, and plan for future study

Not Very Valuable: Meaning and intent are "fuzzy"; feedback is not especially relative and gives me little concrete information about my overall progress or help in planning for improvement of future work

In a summary statement of three sentences or less, I would say rubrics as a social studies assessment tool are:

_____

_____

_____

_____

_____

_____

Assessment Rubric for Using Bloom's Taxonomy to Evaluate a Product, Performance, or Portfolio

Type of Product: _____

Topic: _____

Knowledge: Evidence of learned facts, methods, procedures, or concepts.

| Great Evidence | Ample Evidence | Little Evidence |

Comprehension: Evidence of understanding of facts, methods, procedures, or concepts.

| Great Evidence | Ample Evidence | Little Evidence |

Application: Evidence of use of the information in new situations.

| Great Evidence | Ample Evidence | Little Evidence |

Analysis: Evidence of analysis, recognition of assumptions, and evaluation of relevancy of information.

| Great Evidence | Ample Evidence | Little Evidence |

Synthesis: Evidence of putting information together in a new and creative way.

| Great Evidence | Ample Evidence | Little Evidence |

Evaluation: Evidence of acceptance or rejection of information on the basis of criteria.

| Great Evidence | Ample Evidence | Little Evidence |

Comments by Student: _____

_____

_____

Signed _____ Date _____

Comments by Teacher: _____

_____

_____

Signed _____ Date _____

Standards-Based SOCIAL STUDIES Graphic Organizers, Rubrics, and Writing Prompts for Middle Grade Students

Copyright ©2001 by Incentive Publications, Inc. Nashville, TN.

Cooperative Learning
Group Performance

Topic: _____

Group Members: _____

_____

_____

_____

Date: _____ **Reporter:** _____

Rating Scale: 3 = Outstanding   2 = Satisfactory   3 = Needs Improvement

Rating:

1. Each member of the group contributed ideas and suggestions for setting goals, assigning roles, and developing and carrying out a plan of action.	
2. Each member of our group carried out the duties of his or her role.	
3. Each member of our group exhibited respect for the other members.	
4. Each member of our group exhibited good listening skills and an interest in other group members' contributions.	
5. Each member of the group applied conflict resolution skills as appropriate.	
6. Each member of the group contributed to the content focus and overall performance.	
7. A positive, pleasant, and cheerful atmosphere was maintained during group meetings.	
8. Group goals were achieved.	
9. The overall rating we would give our group is . . .	

*Standards-Based SOCIAL STUDIES Graphic Organizers,
Rubrics, and Writing Prompts for Middle Grade Students*

Questions for Teachers and Students to Consider About Using Rubrics in the Classroom

1. What is a rubric and what kinds of rubrics are there?

   _____

2. What are some characteristics of effective rubrics?

   _____

3. What are the critical components in the design of rubrics?

   _____

4. What is a holistic rubric?

   _____

5. What is an analytical rubric?

   _____

6. Are rubrics developed by students, by teachers, or both?

   _____

7. How does one decide on the criteria of a given rubric?

   _____

8. How does one determine the best type of rating scale for a given rubric?

   _____

9. Are rubrics appropriate for all types of instruction and all types of content areas?

   _____

10. How does one teach students to use and value rubrics as an assessment tool?

    _____

11. Why are rubrics an effective way to measure student performance?

    _____

12. Are rubrics appropriate for measuring the quality of a student-generated product?

    _____

13. How does one translate the results of a rubric into a numerical grade?

    _____

14. How does one use rubrics to guide evaluation and establish a shared standard of quality work?

    _____

15. Are the development and use of rubrics more time consuming for students and teachers as an assessment tool and, if so, is that time commitment worth the effort?

    _____

Appendix

Culture

Social studies programs should include experiences that provide for the study of culture and cultural diversity.

Human beings create, learn, and adapt to culture. Culture helps us to understand ourselves both as individual and as members of various groups. Human cultures exhibit both similarities and differences. We all, for example, have systems of beliefs, knowledge, values, and traditions. Each system also is unique. In a democratic and multicultural society, students need to understand multiple perspectives that derive from different cultural vantage points. This understanding will allow them to relate to people in our nation and throughout the world.

Cultures are dynamic and ever-changing. The study of culture prepares students to ask and answer questions such as: What are the common characteristics of different cultures? How do belief systems, such as religion or political ideas of the culture, influence other parts of the culture? How does the culture change to accommodate different ideas and beliefs? What does language tell us about culture? In schools, this theme typically appears in units and courses dealing with geography, history, and anthropology, as well as multicultural topics across the curriculum.

In the middle grades, students begin to explore and ask questions about the nature of culture and specific aspects of culture, such as language and beliefs, and the influence of those aspects on human behavior.

Source: Curriculum Standards for Social Studies

Culture

Social studies programs should include experiences that provide for the study of culture and cultural diversity so that the middle grades learner can:

1. compare similarities and differences in the ways groups, societies, and cultures meet human needs and concerns.

2. explain how information and experiences may be interpreted by people from diverse cultural perspectives and frames of reference.

3. explain and give examples of how language, literature, the arts, architecture, other artifacts, traditions, beliefs, values, and behaviors contribute to the development and transmission of culture.

4. explain why individuals and groups respond differently to their physical and social environments and/or changes to them on the basis of shared assumptions, values, and beliefs.

5. articulate the implications of cultural diversity, as well as cohesion within and across groups.

Source: Curriculum Standards for Social Studies

Time, Continuity, and Change

Social studies programs should include experiences that provide for the study of how human beings view themselves in and over time.

Human beings seem to understand their historical roots and locate themselves in time. Such understanding involves knowing what things were like in the past and how things will change and develop in the future. Knowing how to read and reconstruct the past allows one to develop a historical perspective and to answer questions such as: Who am I? What happened in the past? How am I connected to those in the past? How has the world changed and how might it change in the future? Why does our personal sense of relatedness to the past change? How can the perspective we have about our own life experiences be viewed as part of the larger human story across time? How do personal stories reflect varying points of view and inform contemporary ideas and actions?

This theme typically appears in courses that: 1) include perspectives from various aspects of history; 2) draw upon historical knowledge during the examination of social issues; and 3) develop the habits of mind that historians and scholars in the humanities and social sciences employ to study the past and its relationship to the present in the United States and other societies.

In the middle grades, students, through a more formal study of history, continue to expand their understanding of the past and of historical concepts and inquiry. They begin to understand and appreciate differences in historical perspectives, recognizing that interpretations are influenced by individual experiences, societal values, and cultural traditions.

Source: Curriculum Standards for Social Studies

Time, Continuity, and Change

Social studies programs should include experiences that provide for the study of the ways human beings view themselves in and over time, so that the middle grades learner can:

1. demonstrate an understanding that different scholars may describe the same event or situation in different ways but must provide reasons or evidence for their views.

2. identify and use key concepts such as chronology, causality, change, conflict, and complexity to explain, analyze, and show connections among patterns of historical change and continuity.

3. identify and describe selected historical periods and patterns of change within and across cultures, such as the rise of civilizations, the development of transportation systems, the growth and breakdown of colonial systems, and others.

4. identify and use processes important to reconstructing and reinterpreting the past, such as using a variety of sources, providing, validating, and weighing evidence for claims, checking credibility of sources, and searching for causality.

5. develop critical sensitivities such as empathy and skepticism regarding attitudes, values, and behaviors of people in different historical contexts.

6. use knowledge of facts and concepts drawn from history, along with methods of historical inquiry, to inform decision-making about and action-taking on public issues.

Source: Curriculum Standards for Social Studies

People, Places, and Environments

Social studies programs should include experiences that provide for the study of people, places, and environments.

Technological advances connect students at all levels to the world. The study of people, places, and human-environment interactions assists learners as they create their spatial views and geographic perspectives of the world. Today's social, cultural, economic, and civic demands on individuals mean that students will need the knowledge, skills, and understanding to ask and answer questions such as: Where are things located? Why are they located where they are? What patterns are reflected in the groupings of things? What do we mean by region? How do landforms change? What implications do these changes have people? This area of study helps learners make informed and critical decisions about the relationship between human beings and their environment. In schools, this theme typically appears in units and courses dealing with area studies and geography.

During the middle school years, students relate their personal experiences to happenings in environmental contexts. Appropriate experiences will encourage increasingly abstract thought as students use data and apply skills in analyzing human behavior in relation to its physical and cultural environment.

Source: Curriculum Standards for Social Studies

People, Places, and Environments

Social studies programs should include experiences that provide for the study of people, places, and environments, so that the middle grades learner can:

1. elaborate mental maps of locales, regions, and the world that demonstrate understanding of relative location, direction, size, and shape.

2. create, interpret, use, and distinguish various representations of the earth, such as maps, globes, and photographs.

3. use appropriate resources, data sources, and geographic tools such as aerial photographs, satellite images, geographic information systems (GIS), map projections, and cartography to generate, manipulate, and interpret information such as atlases, data bases, grid systems, charts, graphs, and maps.

4. estimate distance, calculate scale, and distinguish other geographic relationships such as population density and spatial distribution patterns.

5. locate and describe varying landforms and geographic features, such as mountains, plateaus, islands, rain forests, deserts, and oceans, and explain their relationships within the ecosystem.

6. describe physical system changes such as seasons, climate and weather, and the water cycle and identify geographic patterns associated with them.

7. describe how people create places that reflect cultural values and ideals as they build neighborhoods, parks, shopping centers, and the like.

8. examine, interpret, and analyze physical and cultural patterns and their interactions, such as land use, settlement patterns, cultural transmission of customs and ideas, and ecosystem changes.

9. describe ways that historical events have been influenced by, and have influenced, physical and human geographic factors in local, regional, national, and global settings.

10. observe and speculate about social and economic effects of environmental changes and crises resulting from phenomena such as floods, storms, and drought.

11. propose, compare, and evaluate alternative uses of land and resources in communities, regions, nations, and the world.

Source: Curriculum Standards for Social Studies

Standards-Based SOCIAL STUDIES Graphic Organizers, Rubrics, and Writing Prompts for Middle Grade Students

Individual Development and Identity

Social studies programs should include experiences that provide for the study of individual development and identity.

Personal identity is shaped by one's culture, by groups, and by institutional influences. How do people learn? Why do people behave as they do? What influences how people learn, perceive, and grow? How do people meet their basic needs in a variety of contexts? Questions such as these are central to the study of how individuals develop from youth to adulthood. Examination of various forms of human behavior enhances understanding of the relationships among social norms and emerging personal identities, the social processes that influence identity formation, and the ethical principles underlying individual action. In schools, this theme typically appears in units and courses dealing with psychology and anthropology.

Given the nature of individual development and our own cultural context, students need to be aware of the processes of learning, growth, and development at every level of their school experience. In the middle grades, issues of personal identity are refocused as the individual begins to explain self in relation to others in the society and culture.

Source: Curriculum Standards for Social Studies

Individual Development and Identity

Social studies programs should include experiences that provide for the study of individual development and identity, so that the middle grades learner can:

1. relate personal changes to social, cultural, and historical contexts.

2. describe personal connections to place—as associated with community, nation, and the world.

3. describe the ways family, gender, ethnicity, nationality, and institutional affiliations contribute to personal identity.

4. relate such factors as physical endowment and capabilities, learning, motivation, personality, perception, and behavior to individual development.

5. identify and describe ways regional, ethnic, and national cultures influence individuals' daily lives.

6. identify and describe the influence of perception, attitudes, values, and beliefs on personal identity.

7. identify and interpret examples of stereotyping, conformity, and altruism.

8. work independently and cooperatively to accomplish goals.

Source: Curriculum Standards for Social Studies

Individuals, Groups, and Institutions

Social studies programs should include experiences that provide for the study of interactions among individuals, groups, and institutions.

Institutions such as schools, churches, families, government agencies, and the courts all play an integral role in our lives. These and other institutions exert enormous influence over us, yet institutions are no more than organizational embodiments to further the core social values of those who comprise them. Thus, it is important that students know how institutions are formed, what controls and influences them, how they control and influence individuals and culture, and how institutions can be maintained or changed. The study of individuals, groups, and institutions, prepares students to ask and answer questions such as: What is the role of institutions in this and other societies? How am I influenced by institutions? How do institutions change? What is my role in institutional change? In schools, this theme typically appears in units and courses dealing with sociology, anthropology, psychology, political science, and history.

Middle school learners will benefit from varied experiences as they examine the ways in which institutions change over time, promote social conformity, and influence culture. They should be encouraged to use this understanding to suggest ways to work through institutional change for the common good.

Source: Curriculum Standards for Social Studies

Individuals, Groups, and Institutions

Social studies programs should include experiences that provide for the study of interaction among individuals, groups, and institutions, so that the middle grades learner can:

1. demonstrate an understanding of concepts such as role, status, and social class in describing the interactions of individuals and social groups.

2. analyze group and institutional influences on people, events, and elements of culture.

3. describe the various forms institutions take and the interactions of people with institutions.

4. identify and analyze examples of tensions between expressions of individuality and group or institutional efforts to promote social conformity.

5. identify and describe examples of tensions between belief systems and government policies and laws.

6. describe the role of institutions in furthering both continuity and change.

7. apply knowledge of how groups and institutions work to meet individual needs and promote the common good.

Source: Curriculum Standards for Social Studies

Power, Authority, and Governance

Social studies programs should include experiences that provide for the study of how people create and change structures of power, authority, and governance.

Understanding the historical development of structures of power, authority, and governance and their evolving functions in contemporary U.S. society, as well as in other parts of the world, is essential for developing civic competence. In exploring this theme, students confront questions such as: What is power? What forms does it take? Who holds it? How is it gained, used, and justified? What is legitimate authority? How are governments created, structured, maintained, and changed? How can we keep government responsive to its citizens' needs and interests? How can individual rights be protected within the context of majority rule? By examining the purposes and characteristics of various government systems, learners develop an understanding of how groups and nations attempt to resolve conflicts and seek to establish order and security. Through study of the dynamic relationships among individual rights and responsibilities, the needs of social groups, and concepts of a just society, students become more effective problem-solvers and decision makers when addressing the persistent issues and social problems encountered in public life. They do so buy applying concepts and methods of political science and law. In schools, this theme typically appears in units and courses dealing with government, politics, political science, history, law, and other social sciences.

During the middle school years, these rights and responsibilities are applied in more complex contexts with emphasis on new applications. Middle school students should have opportunities to apply their knowledge and skills to and participate in the workings of the various levels of power, authority, and governance.

Source: Curriculum Standards for Social Studies

Power, Authority, and Governance

Social studies programs should include experiences that provide for the study of how people create and change structures of power, authority, and governance, so that the middle grades learner can:

1. examine persistent issues involving the rights, roles, and status of the individual in relation to the general welfare.

2. describe the purpose of government and how its powers are acquired, used, and justified.

3. analyze and explain ideas and governmental mechanisms to meet needs and wants of citizens, regulate territory, manage conflict, and establish order and security.

4. describe the ways nations and organizations respond to forces of unity and diversity affecting order and security.

5. identify and describe the basic features of the political system in the United States, and identify representative leaders from various levels and branches of government.

6. explain conditions, actions, and motivations that contribute to conflict and cooperation within and among nations.

7. describe and analyze the role of technology in communications, transportation, information processing, weapons development, or other areas as they contribute to or help resolve conflicts.

8. explain and apply concepts such as power, role, status, justice, and influence to the examination of persistent issues and social problems.

9. give examples and explain how governments attempt to achieve their stated ideals at home and abroad.

Source: Curriculum Standards for Social Studies

Production, Distribution, and Consumption

Social studies programs should include experiences that provide for the study of how people organize for the production, distribution, and consumption of goods and services.

People have wants that often exceed the limited resources available to them. As a result, a variety of ways have been invented to decide upon answers to four fundamental questions: What is to be produced? How is production to be organized? How are goods and services to be distributed? What is the most effective allocation of the factors of production (land, labor, capital, and management)? Unequal distribution of resources necessitates systems of exchange, including trade, to improve the well-being of the economy, while the role of government in economic policymaking varies over time and from place to place. Increasingly these decisions are global in scope and require systematic study of an interdependent world economy and the role of technology in economic decision-making. In schools, this theme typically appears in units and courses dealing with concepts, principles, and issues drawn from the discipline of economics.

In the middle grades, learners expand their knowledge of economic concepts and principles, and use economic reasoning processes in addressing issues related to the four fundamental economic questions.

Source: Curriculum Standards for Social Studies

Production, Distribution, and Consumption

Social studies programs should include experiences that provide for the study of how people organize for the production, distribution, and consumption of goods and services, so that the middle grades learner can:

1. give and explain examples of ways that economic systems structure choices about how goods and services are to be produced and distributed.

2. describe the role that supply and demand, prices, incentives, and profits play in determining what is produced and distributed in a competitive market system.

3. explain the difference between private and public goods and services.

4. describe a range of examples of the various institutions that make up economic systems such as households, business firms, banks, government agencies, labor unions, and corporations.

5. describe the role of specialization and exchange in the economic process.

6. explain and illustrate how values and beliefs influence different economic decisions.

7. differentiate among various forms of exchange and money.

8. compare basic economic systems according to who determined what is produced, distributed, and consumed.

9. use economic concepts to help explain historical and current developments and issues in local, national, or global contexts.

10. use economic reasoning to compare different proposals for dealing with a contemporary social issue such as unemployment, acid rain, or high quality education.

Source: Curriculum Standards for Social Studies

Science, Technology, and Society

Social studies programs should include experiences that provide for the study of relationships among science, technology, and society.

Technology is as old as the first crude tool invented by prehistoric humans, but today's technology forms the basis for some of our most difficult social choices. Modern life as we know it would be impossible without technology and the science that supports it. But technology brings with it many questions: Is new technology always better than that which it will replace? What can we learn from the past about how new technologies result in broader social change, some of which is unanticipated? How can we cope with the ever-increasing pace of change, perhaps even with the feeling that technology has gotten out of control? How can we manage technology so that the greatest number of people benefit from it? How can we preserve our fundamental values and beliefs in a world that is rapidly becoming one technology-linked village? This theme appears in units or courses dealing with history, geography, economics, and civics and government. It draws upon several scholarly fields from the natural and physical sciences, social sciences, and the humanities for specific examples of issues and the knowledge base for considering responses to the societal issues related to science and technology.

By the middle grades, students can begin to explore the complex relationships among technology, human values, and behavior. They will find that science and technology bring changes that surprise us and even challenge our beliefs, as in the case of discoveries and their applications related to our universe, the genetic basis of life, atomic physics, and others.

Source: Curriculum Standards for Social Studies

Science, Technology, and Society

Social studies programs should include experiences that provide for the study of relationships among science, technology, and society, so that the middle grades learner can:

1. examine and describe the influence of culture on scientific and technological choices and advancement, such as in transportation, medicine, and warfare.

2. show through specific examples how science and technology have changed people's perceptions of the social and natural world, such as in their relationship to the land, animal life, family life, and economic needs, wants, and security.

3. describe examples in which values, beliefs, and attitudes have been influenced by new scientific and technological knowledge, such as the invention of the printing press, conceptions of the universe, applications of atomic energy, and genetic discoveries.

4. explain the need for laws and policies to govern scientific and technological applications, such as in the safety and well-being of workers and consumers and the regulation of utilities, radio, and television.

5. seek reasonable and ethical solutions to problems that arise when scientific advancements and social norms or values come into conflict.

Source: Curriculum Standards for Social Studies

Global Connections

Social studies programs should include experiences that provide for the study of global connections and interdependence.

The realities of global interdependence require understanding the increasingly important and diverse global connections among world societies. Analysis of tensions between national interests and global priorities contributes to the development of possible solutions to persistent and emerging global issues in many fields: health care, economic development, environmental quality, universal human rights, and others. Analyzing patterns and relationships within and among world cultures, such as economic development, environmental quality, universal human rights, and others. Analyzing patterns and relationships within and among world cultures, such as economic competition and interdependence, age-old ethnic enmities, political and military allowances, and others, helps learners carefully examine policy alternatives that have both national and global implications. This theme typically appears in units or courses dealing with geography, culture, and economics, but again can draw upon the natural and physical sciences and the humanities, including literature, the arts, and language.

In the middle grades, learners can initiate analysis of the interactions among states and nations and their cultural complexities as they respond to global events and changes.

Source: Curriculum Standards for Social Studies

Global Connections

Social studies programs should include experiences that provide for the study of global connections and interdependence, so that the middle grades learner can:

1. describe instances in which language, art, music, belief systems, and other cultural elements can facilitate global understanding or cause misunderstanding.

2. analyze examples of conflict, cooperation, and interdependence among groups, societies, and nations.

3. describe and analyze the effects of changing technologies on the global community.

4. explore the causes, consequences, and possible solutions to persistent, contemporary, and emerging global issues, such as health, security, resource allocation, economic development, and environmental quality.

5. describe and explain the relationships and tensions between national sovereignty and global interests, in such matters as territory, natural resources, trade, use of technology, and welfare of people.

6. demonstrate understanding of concerns, standards, issues, and conflicts related to universal human rights.

7. identify and describe the roles of international and multinational organizations.

Source: Curriculum Standards for Social Studies

Civic Ideals and Practices

Social studies programs should include experiences that provide for the study of the ideals, principles, and practices of citizenship in a democratic republic.

An understanding of civic ideals and practices of citizenship is critical to full participation in society and is a central purpose of the social studies. All people have a stake in examining civic ideals and practices in diverse societies. Learners confront such questions as: What is civic participation and how can I be involved? How has the meaning of citizenship evolved? What is the balance between rights and responsibilities? What is the role of the citizen in the community and the nation, and as a member of the world community? How can I make a positive difference? In schools, this theme typically appears in units or courses dealing with history, political science, cultural anthropology, and fields such as global studies and law-related education, while also drawing upon content from the humanities.

By the middle grades, students expand their ability to analyze and evaluate the relationships between ideals and practice. They are able to see themselves taking civic roles in their communities.

Source: Curriculum Standards for Social Studies

Civic Ideals and Practices

Social studies programs should include experiences that provide for the study of the ideals, principles, and practices of citizenship in a democratic republic, so that the middle grades learner can:

1. examine the origins and continuing influence of key ideals of the democratic republican form of government, such as individual human dignity, liberty, justice, equality, and the rule of law.

2. identify and interpret sources and examples of the rights and responsibilities of citizens.

3. locate, access, analyze, organize, and apply information about selected public issues—recognizing and explaining multiple points of view.

4. practice forms of civic discussion and participation consistent with the ideals of citizens in a democratic republic.

5. explain and analyze various forms of citizen action that influence public policy decisions.

6. identify and explain the roles of formal and informal political actors in influencing and shaping public policy and decision-making.

7. analyze the influence of diverse forms of public opinion on the development of public policy and decision-making.

8. analyze the effectiveness of selected public policies and citizen behaviors in realizing the stated ideals of a democratic republican form of government.

9. explain the relationship between policy statements and action plans used to address issues of public concern.

10. examine strategies designed to strengthen the "common good," which consider a range of options for citizen action.

Source: Curriculum Standards for Social Studies

Planning Matrix

Correlatives: National Social Studies Standards as Identified by the National Council of Social Studies with activities and projects in Standards-Based Graphic Organizers, Rubrics, and Writing Prompts, Incentive Publications, 2001.

Standards	Graphic Organizers	Writing Prompts	Rubrics	Reinforcement & Reflection
Culture	7, 11, 12, 13, 19, 21, 22, 24, 25, 26, 39, 42, 135	47, 48, 49, 50, 136	84, 85, 89, 91, 92, 93, 94, 95, 96, 97, 102, 103, 104, 105, 109	10, 11, 22, 44, 46, 80, 82, 99, 100, 110, 112, 113, 137, 138, 139, 140
Time Continuity & Change	11, 12, 14, 19, 20, 21, 23, 24, 25, 26, 29, 38, 39, 40, 42, 135	51, 52, 53, 136	85, 88, 91, 92, 93, 94, 95, 96, 97, 101, 104, 105	11, 22, 23, 44, 80, 82, 99, 100, 110, 114, 115, 137, 138, 139, 140
People, Places, & Environments	11, 12, 13, 15, 16, 17, 18, 21, 22, 24, 25, 26, 29, 30, 34, 36, 42, 43, 135	60, 61, 62, 136	84, 85, 87, 88, 89, 91, 92, 93, 94, 95, 96, 97, 101, 102, 103, 104, 105, 109	11, 44, 46, 80, 82, 99, 100, 110, 116, 117, 137, 138, 139

Standards-Based SOCIAL STUDIES Graphic Organizers, Rubrics, and Writing Prompts for Middle Grade Students

Planning Matrix

Correlatives: National Social Studies Standards as Identified by the National Council of Social Studies with activities and projects in Standards-Based Graphic Organizers, Rubrics, and Writing Prompts, Incentive Publications, 2001.

Standards	Graphic Organizers	Writing Prompts	Rubrics	Reinforcement & Reflection
Individual Development & Identity	**11, 13, 14, 15, 16, 18, 21, 22, 27, 28, 30, 32, 34, 42, 43, 135**	**67, 68, 136**	**88, 89, 92, 93, 94, 95, 96, 97, 9102, 103, 104, 105, 109**	**44, 46, 80, 82, 99, 100, 106, 107, 120, 121, 137, 138, 139, 140**
Individual Groups & Institutions	**11, 13, 14, 18, 21, 22, 27, 28, 34, 42, 43, 135**	**69, 70, 71, 72, 136**	**87, 88, 92, 93, 94, 95, 96, 97, 102, 103, 104, 105, 109**	**11, 22, 44, 46, 80, 82, 99, 100, 106, 107, 120, 121, 137, 138, 139, 140**
Power, Authority, & Governance	**12, 17, 21, 24, 35, 42, 43, 135**	**54, 55, 56, 136**	**86, 92, 93, 94, 95, 96, 97, 101, 104, 105**	**11, 44, 80, 82, 99, 100, 122, 123, 137, 138, 139, 140**

*Standards-Based SOCIAL STUDIES Graphic Organizers,
Rubrics, and Writing Prompts for Middle Grade Students*

Planning Matrix

Correlatives: National Social Studies Standards as Identified by the National Council of Social Studies with activities and projects in Standards-Based Graphic Organizers, Rubrics, and Writing Prompts, Incentive Publications, 2001.

Standards	Graphic Organizers	Writing Prompts	Rubrics	Reinforcement & Reflection
Production, Distribution, & Consumption	14, 18, 19, 20, 21, 29, 37, 38, 40, 43, 135	57, 58, 59, 136	86, 90, 91, 92, 93, 94, 95, 96, 97, 102, 104, 105	11, 23, 44, 80, 82, 99, 100, 124, 125, 137, 138, 139, 140
Science, Technology, & Society	12, 13, 18, 19, 20, 21, 25, 27, 37, 39, 40, 43, 135	77, 78, 136	86, 90, 93, 94, 95, 96, 97, 98, 99, 104	11, 44, 80, 82, 99, 100, 106, 107, 126, 127, 137, 138, 139, 140
Global Connections	11, 13, 15, 17, 18, 20, 22, 26, 31, 34, 37, 40, 135	73, 74, 75, 76, 136	84, 88, 89, 91, 92, 93, 94, 95, 96, 97, 103, 104, 105	11, 23, 80, 82, 99, 100, 128, 129, 137, 138, 139, 140
Civic Ideals & Practices	11, 12, 15, 16, 18, 19, 21, 23, 24, 31, 33, 34, 38, 42, 135	63, 64, 65, 66, 136	87, 92, 93, 94, 95, 96, 97, 101, 102, 103, 104, 105	11, 23, 44, 80, 82, 99, 100, 130, 131, 137, 138, 139, 140

Suggestions for Using Graphic Organizers to Integrate Social Studies into the Total Curriculum

1. Use concept webs or other advanced organizers to explain scientific ideas as they relate to historical events or current happenings.
   Example: Give a speech on pollution or endangered species.

2. Construct flow charts or diagrams to show processes for completing a specific task related to gathering and disseminating facts and/or information about a social issue of concern to people of your age. *Example:* Use a flow chart to plan and develop a research project on a political or economic concern related to conserving our natural resources for the next generation.

3. Design a puppet show storyboard that shows parts of an important event currently affecting global peace, national security, political stability, or some other topic of social significance. Remember that a storyboard does not attempt to show all of the scenes in a story, but merely serves as an outline for the major people, places, and events.

4. Design a explanatory chart to show an audience the relationships, sequences, or positions that exist within an institution, group, or collection of data. Consider any topic for this chart, from the organization of the various branches of military services, to the types of food chains in natural habitats, to the interactions of fictional characters.

5. Use one or more graphic organizers to prepare a presentation. Some graphic organizers to consider are a Concept Map, a Story Grid, a KWL (Know/Want/Learned) Chart, a Venn diagram, a Web, a Fishbone, or a Matrix. This type of presentation is designed to appeal to a person's ability to reason or to a person's ability to feel emotions. Arrange your arguments so that they:
   (1) ask a question and then answer it;
   (2) relate an anecdote, observation, or experience;
   (3) and state a fact or statistic.

6. Use a Book Report organizer such as the Book Report High-rise on page __ to plan a report on a biography of a famous historical person. As you prepare the report, think about your reactions to the events in the historical figure's life that please or bother you, situations that surprise or dazzle you, and obstacles that challenge or disappoint you.

7. Use Venn diagrams to compare and contrast people, places, and socially significant happenings being studied. *Example:* Compare and contrast the differing opinions of opposing political candidates, economic predictions of financial analysis, cases for and against a proposed highway expansion.

8. Construct line graphs, picot graphs, bar graphs, or circle graphs to organize and present data related to class surveys, research findings, or community poll results.

9. Use time lines to establish the chronology of important events such as the sequence of events leading up to a war, the history of a major social movement such as the civil rights or women's suffrage movement or the life of a famous person.

10. Identify cause and effect situations and construct a cause and effect chart to show the sequence and impact. *Example:* Graphically show the influence of technology in today's schools on the workplace of tomorrow.

Standards-Based SOCIAL STUDIES Graphic Organizers, Rubrics, and Writing Prompts for Middle Grade Students

A Calendar of Journal Prompts to Spark Critical Thinking and Writing

1. Write about what you are doing in class. Consider things that are hard, fun, interesting, confusing, funny, valuable, or challenging. Consider comments about group discussions, homework assignments, independent study options, lectures, or tests/exams.

2. Describe any of the assignments from the teachers using your own words or interpretations.

3. Define specific terms and concepts as you understand or confront them.

4. Compare and contrast two or more assignments, projects, performances, or other learning activities.

5. Explain how to show or perform a specific skill or act.

6. Make realistic guesses about what could have happened if you had done something or some assignment differently.

7. Question what your are learning or doing using a dialogue format.

8. Plan a project or performance with details and expected outcomes.

9. Evaluate your assigned work in a particular class or course.

10. Compose a reaction to something you studied with which you strongly agree or disagree.

11. Paraphrase or summarize a complex idea so that it makes more sense to you.

12. Disclose a reaction to something about which you feel strongly.

13. Build or develop a model, theory, or idea from scratch.

14. Set up an experiment to test a hypothesis.

15. Draw conclusions from a given set of data.

16. Consider an issue or concept from two or more different perspectives.

17. Determine the worth or value of something learned in class.

18. Create a solution to a specific dilemma or problem, or identify the factors or variables that caused a certain decision to be made.

19. Form some generalizations about an assigned topic or problem.

20. Create, compose, design, or develop something new and unique.

21. Complete a series of starter statements such as:

    I wonder . . .

    I wish . . .

    I have learned that . . .

    I need help with . . .

    If only . . .

    I was surprised to find that . . .

Criteria for Creating Your Own Rubric

Excellent

My portfolio, project, or task
1. is complete
2. is well organized
3. is visually exciting
4. shows much evidence of multiple resources
5. shows much evidence of problem solving, decision making, and higher-order thinking skills
6. reflect enthusiasm for the subject
7. contains additional work beyond the requirements
8. communicates effectively what I have learned in keeping with my learning objectives
9. includes highly efficient assessment tools and makes ample provisions for meta cognitive reflection
10. has identified many future learning goals in keeping with my own needs and interests.

Good

My portfolio, project, or task
1. is complete
2. is well organized
3. is interesting
4. shows much evidence of multiple resources
5. shows much evidence of problem solving, decision making, and higher-order thinking skills
6. reflects some interest for the topic
7. contains a small amount of work beyond the requirements
8. communicates what I have learned in keeping with my learning objectives
9. includes effective assessment tools and reflective comments
10. has identified some future learning goals in keeping with my own needs and interests

Needs Improvement

My portfolio, project, or task
1. is incomplete
2. is poorly organized
3. is not very interesting to others
4. shows little or almost no evidence
5. shows little or almost no evidence of problem solving, decision making, and higher-order thinking skills
6. reflects little interest in the subject
7. contains no additional work beyond the minimum requirements
8. communicates few things that I have truly learned in keeping with my objectives
9. includes few examples of self assessment tools and reflective comments
10. has identified no future learning goals in keeping with my own needs and interests.

*Standards-Based SOCIAL STUDIES Graphic Organizers,
Rubrics, and Writing Prompts for Middle Grade Students*

Teacher's
Social Studies Curriculum
Assessment

1. My curriculum plan for the year is well organized to adhere to national and state standards, and to cover all the skills and content mandated for my grade level.

_____   _____   _____   _____
Absolutely   I think so   I hope so   I don't know

Notes/Comments: _____

_____

2. My curriculum plan allows room for meeting individual student needs.

_____   _____   _____   _____
Absolutely   I think so   I hope so   I don't know

Notes/Comments: _____

_____

3. My plan includes a good balance of directed instruction, large and small group work including cooperative learning and flexible groups, and independent study.

_____   _____   _____   _____
Absolutely   I think so   I hope so   I don't know

Notes/Comments: _____

_____

4. Opportunities for student participation and the employment of active learning strategies are prevalent throughout my plan.

_____   _____   _____   _____
Absolutely   I think so   I hope so   I don't know

Notes/Comments: _____

_____

Standards-Based SOCIAL STUDIES Graphic Organizers,
Rubrics, and Writing Prompts for Middle Grade Students

5. I have planned for authentic assessment of student progress as well as for any required traditional methods of assessment such as standardized tests and letter grades where required by the school system.

_____   _____   _____   _____
Absolutely   I think so   I hope so   I don't know

Notes/Comments: _____

_____

_____

---

6. My plan is feasible in terms of time and resources available.

_____   _____   _____   _____
Absolutely   I think so   I hope so   I don't know

Notes/Comments: _____

_____

_____

---

7. I have planned blocks of time to allow flexibility for maximizing those "teachable moments" that encourage spontaneously and foster creativity.

_____   _____   _____   _____
Absolutely   I think so   I hope so   I don't know

Notes/Comments: _____

_____

_____

---

8. My curriculum goals are realistic and achievable yet ambitious in terms of student achievement.

_____   _____   _____   _____
Absolutely   I think so   I hope so   I don't know

Notes/Comments: _____

_____

_____

Standards-Based SOCIAL STUDIES Graphic Organizers, Rubrics, and Writing Prompts for Middle Grade Students

9. My plan provides enrichment activities and time for reflection appropriate to the age level and subject I teach.

    _____   _____   _____   _____

    Absolutely   I think so   I hope so   I don't know

Notes/Comments: _____

_____

10. My plan includes provision for parent communication.

    _____   _____   _____   _____

    Absolutely   I think so   I hope so   I don't know

Notes/Comments: _____

_____

11. My plan is consistent with school goals, administrative expectancies, and will allow for cooperation and partnership with the larger school community.

    _____   _____   _____   _____

    Absolutely   I think so   I hope so   I don't know

Notes/Comments: _____

_____

12. I have reviewed my plan carefully and feel that it is a truly excellent program.

    _____   _____   _____   _____

    Absolutely   I think so   I hope so   I don't know

Notes/Comments: _____

_____

Reflection:

After considering the soundness of my curriculum plan for the year as reflected by this assessment tool, I feel that I should make the following additions, deletions, or modifications.

_____

_____

_____

Date: _____

Standards-Based SOCIAL STUDIES Graphic Organizers, Rubrics, and Writing Prompts for Middle Grade Students

Copyright ©2001 by Incentive Publications, Inc. Nashville, TN.

Bibliography

A to Z Authentic Assessment. Imogene Forte and Sandra Schurr. Nashville, Incentive Publications Inc., 1997.

A to Z Community and Service Learning. Nashville, Incentive Publications Inc., 1997.

BASIC/Not Boring Map Skills Grades 6-8+. Imogene Forte and Marjorie Frank. Nashville, Incentive Publications Inc., 2000.

BASIC/Not Boring Middle Grade Book of Social Studies Tests. Imogene Forte and Marjorie Frank. Nashville, Incentive Publications Inc., 2001.

BASIC/Not Boring U.S. Government, Economics, and Citizenship Grades 6-8+. Imogene Forte and Marjorie Frank. Nashville, Incentive Publications Inc., 1999.

BASIC/Not Boring U.S. History Grades 6-8+. Imogene Forte and Marjorie Frank. Nashville, Incentive Publications Inc., 1997.

BASIC/Not Boring World Geography Grades 6-8+. Imogene Forte and Marjorie Frank. Nashville, Incentive Publications Inc., 1997.

BASIC/Not Boring World History Grades 6-8+. Imogene Forte and Marjorie Frank. Nashville, Incentive Publications Inc., 1997.

Character Education; Grades 6-12 Year One. John Heidel and Marion Lyman-Mersereau. Nashville, Incentive Publications Inc., 1999.

Character Education; Grades 6-12 Year Two. John Heidel and Marion Lyman-Mersereau. Nashville, Incentive Publications Inc., 1999.

The Cooperative Learning Companion. Terri Breeden and Janice Mosley. Nashville, Incentive Publications Inc., 1992.

The Definitive Middle School Guide. Imogene Forte and Sandra Schurr. Nashville, Incentive Publications Inc., 1993.

Graphic Organizers and Planning Outlines. Imogene Forte and Sandra Schurr. Nashville, Incentive Publications Inc., 1996.

How to Write a Great Research Paper. Leland Graham and Darriel Ledbetter. Nashville, Incentive Publications Inc., 1994.

If You're Trying to Teach Kids How to Write, You've Gotta Have this Book! Marjorie Frank. Nashville, Incentive Publications Inc., 1995.

Integrating Instruction in Social Studies. Imogene Forte and Sandra Schurr. Nashville, Incentive Publications Inc., 1996.

Interdisciplinary Units and Projects for Thematic Instruction. Nashville, Incentive Publications Inc., 1994.

Learning to Learn. Gloria Frender. Nashville, Incentive Publications Inc., 1990.

Making Portfolios, Products, and Performances Meaningful and Manageable. Imogene Forte and Sandra Schurr. Nashville, Incentive Publications Inc., 1995.

180 Icebreakers to Strengthen Critical Thinking and Problem-Solving Skills. Imogene Forte and Sandra Schurr. Nashville, Incentive Publications Inc., 1996.

One Nation, 50 States. Imogene Forte. Nashville, Incentive Publications Inc., 1993.

180 Days Around the World. Shirley Cook. Nashville, Incentive Publications Inc., 1993.

Reports Students Love to Write and Teachers Love to Read. Imogene Forte and Sandra Schurr. Nashville, Incentive Publications Inc., 1999.

Social Studies Fair Projects and Research Activities. Darriel Ledbetter and Leland Graham. Nashville, Incentive Publications Inc., 2001.

U.S. Social Studies Yellow Pages. The Kids' Stuff™ People. Nashville, Incentive Publications Inc., 1993.

Use that Computer! Lucinda Johnston, Howard Johnston, and James Forde. Nashville, Incentive Publications Inc., 2001.

World Social Studies Yellow Pages. The Kids' Stuff™ People. Nashville, Incentive Publications Inc., 1993.

Wow, What a Team! Randy Thompson and Dorothy VanderJagt. Nashville, Incentive Publications Inc., 2001.

Index